Copyright 2013 – Kevin Deane

Scripture quotations are from The Holy Bible, English Standard Version® (ESV®), copyright © 2001 by Crossway, a publishing ministry of Good News Publishers. Used by permission. All rights reserved.

Special Thanks:

To Jordan Gold, whose edifying conversations and late-night chats inspired me to begin writing this book. And to Raquel Schmidt, whose searching questions and deepening friendship inspired me to finish it.

Thanks to Kyla Wiebe, for the beautiful cover art, and a beautiful friendship. For more information about her art, you can contact her at kylawiebe@gmail.com

And thanks to Glenn Deane, Andrew Porter and Samuel Katchikian for their wisdom, insight and thoughts on the book. Thank you also to my parents, for their love and support, and to my Dad, who thought of the title.

## Table of Contents

Preface – A Word For You..................................................9

1 – We Are At War............................................................11

2 – My Own Funeral........................................................19

3 – A Living People..........................................................29

4 – Meaningless................................................................41

5 – You Don't Have it Because You Don't Want it......49

6 – You Want Me To Look Like What?!......................59

7 – The Torn Veil.............................................................75

8 – Giving Back................................................................87

9 – Alive In Christ............................................................95

10 – Be Filled With the Spirit.......................................109

11 – Dying to Live..........................................................123

"This is the message we have heard from him and proclaim to you, that God is light, and in him is no darkness at all. If we say we have fellowship with him while we walk in darkness, we lie and do not practice the truth. But if we walk in the light, as he is in the light, we have fellowship with one another, and the blood of Jesus his Son cleanses us from all sin. If we say we have no sin, we deceive ourselves, and the truth is not in us. If we confess our sins, he is faithful and just to forgive us our sins and to cleanse us from all unrighteousness."

1 John 1:5-9


"And we all, with unveiled face, beholding the glory of the Lord, are being transformed into the same image from one degree of glory to another. For this comes from the Lord who is the Spirit."

2 Corinthians 3:18

# Preface: A Word for you (Yes, you!)

> O preacher, holy man, hear my heart weeping:
> I long to stand and shout my protests:
> Where is your power? And where is your message?
> Where is the Gospel of mercy and love?
> Your words are nothingness! Nothingness! Nothingness!
> We who have come to listen are betrayed.
>
> Servant of God, I am bitter and desolate.
> What do I care for perfection of phrase?
> Cursed be your humor, your poise, your diction.
> See how my soul turns to ashes within me.
> You who have vowed to declare your Redeemer,
> Give me the words that would save!

-Margaret Chaplin Anderson[1]

The Bible is the most unique book on the planet. It is the only book written by God Himself, and it contains all that could ever be needed for life – true life. All philosophy from every human thinker of every age combined has never amounted to the wisdom contained within the Scriptures. God Himself has spoken, and mankind is left with the simple responsibility of listening. For that reason, I ask you to listen most carefully to the words of the Bible verses quoted in this book. Please do not skim over or skip verses in this book – even familiar ones, for they are the Words of life from God Himself. Study them, meditate on them, and listen to them. My prayer is that this book is not merely a product of Biblical study, but a resource that encourages you to delve deeper into the Bible for yourself. May it be a tool that drives you further into the study of Scripture.

Let me lay this out for you. In the book of John, Jesus is called 'The Word.' Now I'm not trying to take you back to elementary school, but what is a word? (That's right!) It is our primary means of communication. We write with words, we speak with words. The opposite of words is just blankness, or silence. Jesus, the Living Word, is not silent. He is always speaking, and I want you to know that He has

---

[1] Anderson, Margaret. 'Wail of a Distressed Soul.'

something to say to *you*. I don't know who you are, and I don't know where you're from; I don't know your age, your background, your troubles, your past. I don't know about your habits or addictions (whether its to TV or cocaine), I don't know anything about your prayer and devotional life. But I want you to know that God does know exactly who you are. He knows just exactly how much you do or do not know about Him and His Word, and He knows just exactly how much you do or do not want to be reading this book. And God is always speaking. He never wastes opportunities to say something, and it is my firm conviction that He has something to say to *you* through this book.

I was a camp counsellor for many years, and I always asked my campers the same question. Why are you here? They always had different answers, 'My mom brought me,' or 'Grandma made me come,' and there was always one kid who would say he 'wanted to learn more about the Bible.' And as soon as that kid spoke, then everyone after him wanted to learn about the Bible too. But I would always tell my kids the same thing. 'Yes, you are here because your mom or your grandma brought you, or whatever your reason is. That is true. But I want to suggest another reason to you as well. You are here, because God wants you to be here. You are here, because God has something to say to you.' And I want to suggest the same of this book. I don't know why you're here. I don't know why you're reading, but I would suggest to you that God wants you here. He has something to say to *you*. Right from the creation of the world we see God as a God of order. And I don't mean to open a debate about God's sovereignty, but I don't believe it is any accident you are holding this book.

## Chapter 1: We Are at War

I heard a story once, of a woman who volunteered to help on a work day at her church. She joined the army of women wielding dusters, mops and vacuums as they spent the day scaring away all the exciting things that grow behind pews. This particular woman grabbed her vacuum cleaner and started to push it back and forth over the carpet. As she cleaned, she outran the length of the stretched cord and while thrusting it forward and back, she inadvertently unplugged it from the wall. The afternoon wore on, and as the other women finished, they began to switch off their vacuum cleaners. As the hum of cleaning slowly died, and the other church ladies began to file home, this woman, for the first time all day, noticed that her vacuum was not making any noise. She began to investigate, and it didn't take long, until she discovered the issue. It hadn't been plugged in.

In many ways, we can be like that woman. Not just that we don't notice things that should be really obvious. Although I do that too. But this lady worked a whole afternoon and did...nothing. She started off well – filled with power and purpose. But by the time she reached the end of the day, she was powerless. She went to the church to serve Jesus and accomplished...nothing. And that's often the way we are. Slaving away amidst the noise of fellow believers. Serving Jesus with (so to speak) nothing more than an unplugged vacuum cleaner. All the right action, but without any power.

The church in the New Testament was filled with vibrant, passionate men. Peter, Paul and the other Christians didn't really have much. But they had hearts filled with the Holy Spirit, and lives committed to preaching the gospel. And they turned the world upside down! Its like they weren't just serving Jesus with a vacuum cleaner that was plugged in – they were pushing vacuums with all four limbs.

And sometime I wonder why I'm not doing the same. Why I'm living my life, and seeing so few of my friends converted. Why godliness, and holiness and purity are so hard. Paul never had a finished copy of the Bible, but I do. Most churches require a few thousand dollars worth of sound equipment before they can have an acceptable worship service, but Paul, without a cent to his name, accomplished twice as much. I often feel like I'm pushing an unplugged vacuum, and just adding to the noise of so many other people doing the same thing. Serving the Lord without any true power.

Let's be honest – there are a lot of 'Christian' things going on around us all the time. A pretty significant portion of North America claims to be Christian, and all together, that many people can create a lot of pretty Christiany things: music, movies, conferences, big churches. Its amazing to realize that we, at this moment, have more Bibles than ever before in the history of the world. More Christian books. More Christian music. More speakers. More conferences. Hundreds of opportunities to be taught until we can rattle off the books of the Bible, and hundred and fifty-two reasons why atheists are wrong. Hundreds of opportunities to get excited, and all pumped up at emotional worship services. I'm not trying to say that any of that is bad, I'm just stating some facts. We are some very privileged people with lots of opportunities to do a lot of really cool things.

There are preachers and pastors who would see all the activity going on in the church and all the people filling the pews and be happy. Some Christians would be content to sit back in the nice home God has blessed them with, praise the Lord, give thanks and continue to live a nice life, avoiding sex, drugs and alcohol. Maybe even listen to Christian radio stations. Maybe that's you. Living day to day with an attitude that believes 'I art reasonably holyish.'

But did God make us so we could sit around and do nothing for Him? Paul didn't live a Christian life like we do. He lived a life with power. A spiritual power, that poured out of Him and transformed the lives of countless thousands he came into contact with. He didn't need to go to any pastors' conventions to learn how to get excited about preaching. He walked with God, and God so filled His heart that it permeated every word he spoke.

Quite often we look around at one another, see others living the same way we are and are satisfied with our level of godliness. We go to church each Sunday and grow in our knowledge of God, but not in our desire to see the gospel taken to the nations, not in our hatred of sin, and not in our understanding of eternity. Personally, I often find myself forgetting the reality of eternity, and catch myself sitting back, living a mediocre Christian life while our country walks into Hell. When we begin to adapt to our culture and its mindset - something the Bible warns against countless times - we are no longer soldiers of the cross, but an army without weapons Our society is incredibly tolerant of any mindset or lifestyle - we all encounter this attitude on a regular basis. However, Christ has called us to come after Him daily by standing against the current of this age. We aren't to be content with ungodliness and accepting of sin, but we are to make a bold stance for His Kingdom. We are to live the way He desired us to – in holiness – and boldly declare war on that which stands against our God and our King.

**For we do not wrestle against flesh and blood, but against the rulers, against the authorities, against the cosmic powers over this present darkness, against the spiritual forces of evil in the heavenly places. (Ephesians 6:12)**

In the 1980's Dr. A. W. Tozer challenged the church with the question, "Is this world a playground or a battleground?"[2] I remember in elementary school I came into the principal's office and saw a kid who had started a fight because another kid made fun of his expensive shoes. The world looks on and mocks my God, His church and His word – all infinitely more valuable than a pair of shoes. How can I sit back and be comfortable? Is this a playground or a battleground? The Bible calls us soldiers. Shall we sit and be silent about eternal issues, but rise to fight when someone mocks our shoes?

We are to be soldiers, making an emphatic stand for holiness and purity. We are to be living with the fullness of God in our hearts, so that when the world looks at us, they see Jesus and are amazed.

**"Let your light shine before others, so that they may see your good works and give glory to your Father who is in heaven." (Matthew 5:16)**

---

2       Tozer, A.W. *This World: Playground or Battleground?* Camp Hill, PA: Christian Publications, 1988. Print.

Martyn Lloyd Jones once said, "People seem to think that the masses are outside the Christian church because our evangelistic methods are not what they ought to be. That is not the answer. People are outside the church because looking at us they say, 'What is the point of being Christians? - look at them!' They are judging Christ by you and me. And you cannot stop them and you cannot blame them."

We were told to go into the world and make disciples – men and women who look and act like Christ. But quite often the world comes into the church and makes disciples of us – men and women who look and act like everybody else.

So I write this book in opposition to that. I want the body of believers to set aside the ways of the world and rise to the fullness of the life God has called us to. Regardless of where you are spiritually, we should never stop in our pursuit of God, so I want to encourage you to seek less of self and more of God. If you are in a youth group or a church, there are hundreds of opportunities for you to be encouraged and told that God loves you and that He will take care of your needs. Praise the Lord for the privilege of living in a free country where you can be reminded of truths like that, but may this book serve to remind you that this world is not a playground. It is a battleground, and we are soldiers. I have no interest in writing well-crafted words if the world will just look at us, shake their heads, and walk into hell. I desire to be a soldier that people will recognize as a follower of Christ. Paul says this to Timothy:

**"Train yourself for godliness; for while bodily training is of some value, godliness is of value in every way, as it holds promise for the present life and also for the life to come. Let no one despise you for your youth, but set the believers an example in speech, in conduct, in love, in faith, in purity." (1 Timothy 4:7b-8, 12)**

I wrote this book because I want to see people come to life. I want to see living examples of what love, faith and purity are supposed to look like. I long to see people develop even further into passionate, sacrificial servants of Jesus Christ. I want to see men and women rise up, take up their crosses and live out the reality of a risen Lord. The same Spirit that filled Paul's heart has been offered to you. There is no measure of spiritual power being withheld from you. What would it be like if high school students across the country were filled the Holy Spirit and proclaimed the gospel with boldness?

Because you're representing Jesus' gospel, the way you live will testify to how powerful the cross really is. Your words and actions in everyday life will demonstrate how radically Jesus is able to change a life. We are to live out the reality that Jesus died to save us from sin and rose from the dead to give new life.

Saint Francis of Assisi was always credited with saying (although whether or not he actually said it is another question): "Preach the Gospel always, and if necessary, use words." And that's what this is all about. Living out the Christianity that we have seen in the Bible until we reach the point where we are proclaiming Jesus' name everywhere we go by the godliness of our words and actions. (Just as a little side note, don't get too carried away with the thought of only using words when necessary – Jesus commanded us to proclaim the gospel, so don't think you'll get away without ever using words.)

Jesus didn't come to Earth just to feed the poor, to encourage people, or to solve their financial problems. He may very well do all that, but His primary purpose in coming was to bring dead men (sinners) to life. To save us from sin. Not just from its penalty, but from the present grip it has on our lives.

So I don't want to see young people being encouraged, taught and excited. If, while reading this book, you get those three things, that's wonderful. But the primary goal is to see people like you living out the reality of a Saviour that has conquered death and sin. Living with hearts that are defined by the Holy One of Israel – the God that created the world, split the red sea, threw fire down on Mt. Carmel and rushed like a wind at Pentecost. We were called to be like Christ. We were called to be alive. Not just smart and with good self-esteem, but passionate and sacrificial. Let's take our Bibles (our swords) and get on our knees and fight like the soldiers we were called to be. Jesus said:

**"On this rock I will build my church, and the gates of hell shall not prevail against it." (Matthew 16:18)**

I think sometimes we forget that 'gates' are a defensive weapon. We are the ones that are supposed to be attacking hell. But often times it feels as though hell is attacking us. It's not just what you believe that is important, but what you will believe with such urgency that it will change your life. The purpose of the church isn't just to improve the moral standing of a culture but to be radically transformed by the message of the cross.

Christ has died, saved us from sin, and we rise up, clothed in His righteousness, to live out that reality. He's done it, but we choose to live it. We can all say that we're righteous. Or we can all point fingers at every other church or every other person, wag our heads, and say 'how dare they be so sinful.' We can all talk like Christians. But are you *living* it? Are you living, truly living, saved from sin, in a passionate, daily pursuit of God, or are you still bound by fear, and lust and pride? Are you being conformed to the world or being transformed by the renewing of your mind? Are you gaining the whole world, or are you surrendering your soul? Are you making disciples of all people and teaching them to obey all that the Lord commanded, or is everyone around you ignorant of Christ, and teaching you to ignore what they believe to be irrelevant laws?

What does it look like for a person to fully live the 'born-again' life Jesus promised? I think Paul is a fine example of just what the new life is all about. I mean, have you considered this man's life? He meets Jesus one day, repents, leaves his old life behind, and from that moment on, lives in the new life Christ has given him. He would stop at nothing to preach the gospel. Everywhere he went, daily, he was giving up everything he had for the cause of Christ.

**"Five times I received at the hands of the Jews the forty lashes less one. Three times I was beaten with rods. Once I was stoned. Three times I was shipwrecked; a night and a day I was adrift at sea; on frequent journeys, in danger from rivers, danger from robbers, danger from my own people, danger from Gentiles, danger in the city, danger in the wilderness, danger at sea, danger from false**

**brothers; in toil and hardship, through many a sleepless night, in hunger and thirst, often without food, in cold and exposure. And, apart from other things, there is the daily pressure on me of my anxiety for all the churches." (2 Corinthians 11:24-27)**

He was filled with the Spirit, and though he once hated Christ, he was now proclaiming the gospel. Just by being beaten and stoned and never giving up, He demonstrated what joy and worth there is in following Christ. And that's what you are called to do. There has definitely been more than one point in my Christian walk, when I just got sick of living an average, lukewarm Christian life like everyone else. I was alive, spiritually, but I wasn't living out that reality. If we are really going to call ourselves followers of Christ, we need to be like Paul – living in radical devotion for Jesus. One life, sold out entirely for the gospel, and he turned the world upside down. Let's be willing to take the persecution, the shame, for the sake of Christ. This book was not written so you can read and continue to live like everyone else in your church. We weren't called to be like others.

Paul is a wonderful New Testament picture of Christian living. He is the kind of Christian Jesus was talking about. Jesus never told you to build a big church and argue about theology. But He has told you, like He told Lazarus, to come alive. Because, as much as I love the church in this country, and I really do love the church, sometimes its really hard to distinguish between the light and the dark. I don't know about you, but I'm dying to live. So, Christian young people, lets stop being mediocre. Lets go live for a God worth living for, and if need be, die for Him, because He is worth dying for. We have been given new life, and a Spirit of power, so let us live like that is the case. This is world is a battleground. Be a soldier.

*Dear Father,*
*You have called us to live lives completely sold out to you.*
*So often I feel like I'm going through the motions of Christian living,*
*but there is no power.*
*Reignite in me a passion for your name.*
*Remind me that this world is a battleground and not a playground.*

*I don't just want to add to the noise of Christianity,*
*I want to be accomplishing something for your glory.*
*Make me a soldier.*
*In Jesus name,*
*Amen.*

## Chapter 2: My own funeral

I don't know where you're at spiritually, and quite frankly it doesn't matter. Throughout the book of Leviticus, God continues hammering this one command into His people: "Be Holy, for I am Holy (Leviticus 11:44, 11:45, 19:2, 20:7, 20:26, 21:8, quoted in 1 Peter 1:16)." In many ways it is the underlying purpose of the entire law.

God says to be holy, but we aren't very good at actually being holy. At least, I'm not. I know I'm not qualified to judge your life, or anyone else, but I assume there are at least a few other people in the world like me. I know that I'm really good at going to conferences and camps and retreats and getting all pumped up for God and seeing a passion that burns for maybe a week. And I feel like I'm not alone. I don't have to talk to very many of my camp counsellors before I meet others who can lead Bible studies, but still find themselves bound to so many besetting sins. We are really good at hammering into our campers to be holy, and talking at youth group about avoiding sin, and failing utterly at home alone in front of the computer.

We'll talk more about holiness in chapter 7, but the point is that sometimes its hard to live for Christ. Even though we usually don't want to admit it out loud, it can be hard to love Him, and to want to serve Him. If you sincerely wanted to love and serve Him *all* the time, you would never sin. So how do we live the Christian life? How do live righteously in the middle of a world that throws sin at us from all sides? How can I have a heart that actually wants to live for God?

I believe the secret is in understanding the difference between death and life.

The moment a person is saved is the moment that they put their faith in the saving power of the finished work of the cross of Jesus Christ. They identify themselves with His death, and what the Bible calls 'the flesh' - their lusting, proud, sin-loving inner nature - is crucified with Him. The part of them that likes sin is put to death. And just as He rose victorious over sin, so the believer is given a new life. They are born again, and from that moment on they ought to begin growing in their hatred for the things of sin they once loved, and in their love for the things of God they were once indifferent towards. To put that more simply, Christ's death was your death too – every part of you that loves sin died with Him. And His resurrection was your resurrection too – the life you live is now lived to the glory of God.

**"I have been crucified with Christ. It is no longer I who live, but Christ who lives in me. And the life I now live in the flesh I live by faith in the Son of God, who loved me and gave himself for me." (Galatians 2:20)**

But there are times in our lives (like high school) when our defences are down, and our daily thirst for God slowly dries up. There is a spiritual 'lull' that occurs – a dullness of the heart - and as sin begins to creep back in, the new believer that was once passionate for the Kingdom begins to fall back into a spiritual sleep. They begin to no longer live in the new life Christ gave them., but start to come to a place where they love other things - like money, a boyfriend/girlfriend or (most often) themselves - more than they love God. If you're like most Christians, you've probably found yourself for periods of time forgetting the two greatest commandments,

**"You shall Love the Lord your God with all your heart, soul, strength and mind." (Deuteronomy 6:5, Matthew 22:37, Mark 12: 30, Luke 10:27)**

and

**"Love your neighbour as yourself." (Leviticus 19:8, Matthew 22:39 Mark 12:31, Luke 10:27)**

The flesh, sin-loving nature that Christ did away with when you were converted, rises again, and we find ourselves living the true Christian life conditionally. What I mean by that is, that when I sing the songs about Jesus being my everything, I mean it. At the time. But ten minutes later I'm back to loving myself more than God. At camp, and at church and in youth group I love Jesus, but when it comes to the day by day, moment by moment battle, the flesh continually wins. We live a life of constantly letting other things (relationships, sports, plans for the future) be more important than God. His resurrection was supposed to be our resurrection too, but we so easily slip into a life that is not, to the full extent, being lived by faith in the Son of God that loved us and gave Himself up for us. Instead, you will find yourself living for yourself. Sleeping in, rather than doing morning devotions (as one example), because you love your own comfort more than God. So what do we need to do? We need to begin at place where we recognize our own powerlessness.

Let me tell you a story. I was working as a counsellor at a camp during a January weekend, when there was a knock on my cabin door. A girl a few years older than myself stood outside, asking to speak to me. I put my campers to bed, and, finding a public lounge, this girl began to tell me her story. I don't remember all the details, but she began to explain to me how her life had fallen apart. Her only friend in the world had left her, her parents had kicked her out, her boyfriend had raped her, and she had gotten on a plane, flown across the country, and found her way to this camp she had once been to. She recognized me as the son of a preacher she had once heard and came to me, desperately asking where God was in all of this. What was God's will? What was His plan? How was she to live for God in the midst of these shambles?

So I told her the same thing I've told every person who has ever asked me how to live their life for God.

Give up.

In other words, surrender. You can't do it. You just can't. You can try, and I promise you, you will fail. You will never understand the life God has called you to as long as you're trying to do everything yourself. I think often we spend our Christian walks fighting for something that has already been given to us. For free. The grace and the strength and the guidance she needed for that situation had already been offered to her, but she was trying so hard to do well on her own, there was no room for Jesus' help. He can't help you when you're trying to do everything yourself.

**"And when Jesus heard it, he said to them, 'Those who are well have no need of a physician, but those who are sick. I came not to call the righteous, but sinners.'" (Mark 2:17)**

Before you can go anywhere, you need to realize you can't go anywhere on your own. If you believe yourself to be righteous, Jesus can't do anything for you. Before the Great Physician will tend to you, you must realize that you are sick. You must admit your need. You must give up your own efforts. In fact, you must lay down everything. You wonder why a passion for God is not filling your heart? Because your heart is already filled with passion for other things. Before you can be filled, you must be emptied entirely.

It's like this: the first vehicle I ever owned was a 1989 Ford Econoline 150 - one of those box vans that plumbers use. The most retro van any college student could possibly purchase. I split the cost of it with 8 friends and we painted it up like our favourite football team. If you ever make a really good group of friends in college, I sincerely recommend purchasing a van together. It had swivel seats and a bench that folded into a bed and seven whole seat belts, although six didn't work. And no, sadly, it did not have shag carpet. On our very first excursion, we fit a grand total of 32 people into the van. Now 32 people filling out seven (one) seat belts makes things rather...squishy. And every single person in our college wanted a ride in the new van. But it didn't matter how willing we were to take in new people, there was just no way to cram another soul into that beautifully majestic van.

Catching the similarities? It doesn't matter how badly you want to 'cram' God into your life, nor what your willing to do in order to get Him into your life. If your passions are burning for the things of this world and your dedication is spent following after those passions, you truly have *no* more room to fit God in. All the things in your life that you love are like 32 sweaty individuals in a van with swivel seats.

**"Whoever loves father or mother more than me is not worthy of me, and whoever loves son or daughter more than me is not worthy of me. And whoever does not take up his cross and follow me is not worthy of me." (Matthew 10:37-38)**

I already mentioned that the greatest commandment in the Bible is to love the Lord your God with all your heart, soul strength and mind. That also happens to be the most meaningful and beneficial lifestyle you can have. Are you doing that? Are you loving Him with everything? I think on an average read of that passage, I kind of just assume that I am. 'Jesus? Oh, I love him.' But when did love become unmoving? When did love not consume a person's life? Sometime, go watch a 13 year old boy in love with a girl. He'll flip cartwheels to get her attention! And that's when he doesn't even know her! You actually really have to stretch the definition of the word love to even call a 13 year old crush 'love.' Yet, most of the time it looks far more like love than our actions and attitudes before God.

**By this we know love, that he laid down His life for us, and we ought to lay our lives down for our brothers." (1 John 3:16)**

According to this verse, love is demonstrated by a willingness to lay itself down to die for another person. Do you love God? We're told all the time that God loves us. Jesus loves you. What a glorious truth! But what is your response? Do you love Him in return? If you're honest (and you're like me), probably not. Other things creep into our lives so easily. Its hard to *want* to go to church (even if we do go), and yet we rush to the theatre to watch the latest blockbuster. We spend a couple hours each week talking to friends on facebook, and only a few minutes talking to God. Video games are more captivating than Bible reading.

The list of things that we love more than God goes on and on, and differs for every person, but the point remains. We all at some point come to the place where our joy is not found in God. I so appreciate the very honest song:

"I need to just admit
My faith is paper thin
I'm feeling so burned out
On religion

I say an empty prayer
I sing a tired song
I need to just admit that the passion's gone"[3]

---

[3]    Starfield. "Rediscover You." *The Saving One*. Sparrow Records, 2010. CD.

Though we were once raised from spiritual death the way Lazarus was raised from physical death, we once again find ourselves bound and gagged by the same grave clothes we wore when we were dead. Sometimes I meet Christians living sinful lives wondering why they don't know the will of God. They've come to resemble the spiritually dead and don't realize that dead men can't hear!

Truth is, if you have absolutely no desire to live for God any more than you are now, I really can't help you. You might as well just put this book down, because if you have no interest in growing closer with God, you never will. In fact, having a desire to grow closer with Him, is evidence that you are born again, because spirit gives birth to spirit - so if you have no desire to grow closer with God, there is no evidence you are actually a true Christian. And if you *are* born again and have that desire, but choose not to act upon it, I still can't help you. If you want to love your boy/girlfriend more than God, you are actually the only one who can do anything to change that. I'll just leave that between you and Him.

The Gospel has no power to save the self-righteous, for Christ did not come into the world to heal the healthy, but the sick. Likewise, God does not continue to fill the cups and hearts of believers who believe themselves to be fully satisfied. If you think you have the full extent of godliness in your life, that you know Him as well as you ever will, then you will stay right where you are.

This is why I say, 'give up.' You want to find God? You want to live a life for Him? Give up. If you don't need Him, you won't have Him. Simple as that. Where do we find freedom from sin? When we admit our own powerlessness, and realize He has lived victoriously on our behalf. He won't free you from sin until you're so surrendered in His arms that you are willing to take and nail yourself to the same cross He hung on.

**"We know that our old self was crucified with him in order that the body of sin might be brought to nothing, so that we would no longer be enslaved to sin. For one who has died has been set free**

**from sin. Now if we have died with Christ, we believe that we will also live with him." (Romans 6:6-8)**

Quite simply, when Jesus died, that was your death too. When you put faith in Him, you are willingly submitting to being hauled away from everything you are and have. What is the secret to living the life that God has called you to live? To die. To claim for ourselves what Paul commands us to do:

**"So you also must consider yourselves dead to sin and alive to God in Christ Jesus." (Romans 6:11)**

Imagine for a moment, if you were to die right now. Imagine if an angel, or some other heavenly being were to swoop down to where you are sitting at this moment, and begin to haul you away to heaven. That isn't in any way what it looks like to die, but just imagine it for a moment, for the sake of the illustration. You're being hauled off this earth right now. Hauled away from your plans for this evening, away from your romantic interests, away from your dreams for the future, away from everything and everyone you love. That is what death would be like for you. A definitive separation from everything you presently know and care about. And according to the Bible it is only when we die with Christ that we will find new life.

**"So you also must consider yourselves dead to sin and alive to God in Christ Jesus. Let not sin therefore reign in your mortal body, to make you obey its passions. Do not present your members to sin as instruments for unrighteousness, but present yourselves to God as those who have been brought from death to life, and your members to God as instruments for righteousness. For sin will have no dominion over you, since you are not under law but under grace." (Romans 6:11-14)**

You want to understand the life God has called you to? You will need to understand the death that crucifies you. If you are a Christian, then when Jesus died, you died with Him. And when you find yourself in a place where you do not love God with all your heart, soul, strength and mind, you must put to death everything that you love more than God.

There must be a permanent separation between your heart and the things it loves more than God. Like an angel dragging you away, you must consciously step away from all that you love and choose to love Christ instead. Just as we repented on the day of salvation and turned from sin, laying down our old habits, ambitions and dreams for the joy of the Lord, so again we must lay down who we are and lay claim of the life Christ has given. Until there is a death of ourselves, there will never be new life, for life only rises from death. A kernel of wheat must fall to the ground and die before it will bring forth a harvest. Jesus once said,

**"Truly, truly, I say to you, unless a grain of wheat falls into the earth and dies, it remains alone; but if it dies, it bears much fruit. Whoever loves his life loses it, and whoever hates his life in this world will keep it for eternal life." (John 12:24-25)**

The day you were saved, you were crucified with Christ. If you truly were saved, your life was permanently altered. Your passions, desires and lifestyle will never be the same. And you are being called to live on that cross. On that cold, inelegant, rough Roman device. There's nothing showy or beautiful about a cross – it only has one purpose: to kill people. You are called to live crucified. To live dying.

It is time to die again. Put to death your sinful habits. Your lusts and temptations, your joys in sin. Put to death the love for yourself, and the things you love more than God. Put to death the love you have for your righteousness. Put to death the fact that you read your Bible and go to church. Put to death the fact you know the songs, you lead the Bible studies, you pray and whatever else. Ask God to search you, and find the pride in your life. And then crucify it. Step away from it forever – just as dying would make you step away from your life forever. Let all that you love be dead to you, and love God.

The psalmist writes this as a cry to God:

**Will you not revive us again,**
**that your people may rejoice in you? Psalm 85:6**

The Psalmist is crying out, asking that he (and the rest of Israel) would come back to the place where their joy was found in the Lord. And we should be crying the same. Because of our sinful nature there is almost a daily need to come back to a place self-death on the cross. You can't love God with all your heart, soul, strength and mind if you love other things. All the things in this world that your heart loves or find joy in must die, in order to make room for a Christ-centred love.

**"And [Jesus] said to all, 'If anyone would come after me, let him deny himself *daily* and follow me. For whoever would save his life will lose it, but whoever loses it for my sake will save it.'" (Luke 9:23-24, emphasis added.)**

You were called to be united with Christ's death – to join Him on the cross – and crosses do not lose. Crosses were meant to kill people, and they were 100% effective. No criminal, no matter how strong, ever crawled down from a cross. The cross always won. Even the Lord Himself died upon the cross. Put yourself to death upon the cross that does not lose. There is power in the cross, and if you want to live, you must die.

When you read about some of Israel's kings in the Old Testament, you'll find good kings and bad kings. Kings that loved God and worshipped Him in the temple, and kings that built altars for other gods. Sometimes God-fearing kings like Josiah or Asa came to power immediately after a wicked king, so the land was still full of idols. They didn't just leave all those idols up and start going to the temple. They knew that turning to God meant turning from idols, and anything that could be a distraction from the true God. If you are going to be serious about seeking God, you must, like Josiah and Asa, tear down everything that distracts. Only you aren't tearing down pagan idols with your hands, you are taking things in your heart that bring you joy, and nailing them (figuratively) to the cross.

As Jim Cymbala wrote, "The first step in any spiritual awakening is *demolition*. We cannot make headway into seeking God without first tearing down accumulated junk in our souls. Rationalizing has to cease. We have to start seeing the sinful debris we hadn't noticed before, which is what holds back the blessings of God. I wonder if any government employee said, 'Excuse me, King Asa, but your father built that particular shrine...Your grandfather dedicated that incense altar...Asa would have replied, 'Tear them down – now! They're wrong...God will never bless us as long as these things stand.[4]

Give up. Surrender. Pray that God would reveal to you what it means to be crucified with Christ.

**"Humble yourselves before the Lord, and he will exalt you." (James 4:10)**

*Dear Father,*

*I can't live a holy Christian life on my own.*

*I need your power to come and resurrect me.*

*Help me to approach the cross the way you intended me to.*

*I desire to live for you,*

*I realize I must pick up my cross and die daily to do so.*

*I lay down my passions, my dreams, my desires, and my pride.*

*Bring me back to the place where I love you with all my heart, soul, strength and mind.*

*Empty me of myself that I might be filled with the joy of knowing you.*

*I will live for you.*

*Let me live crucified with Christ.*

*In Jesus name,*

*Amen*

---

[4] Cymbala, Jim *Fresh Wind Fresh Fire*. Grand Rapids, MI: Zondervan, 2003. Print. p. 159.

## Chapter 3: A Living People

I don't think anything has damaged the church more than the teaching that you can be saved and continue to live precisely as you had been before. This concept is floating around that you can have Jesus as your Saviour and not be radically changed. I want to say this really carefully, because I'm not trying to bash the church today, or tear down every evangelist or well-meaning pastor. I think there are a lot of genuine Christians out there really sincerely seeking to live and preach as the Scriptures have intended us to. I'm not trying to say that every church out there is falsely teaching the gospel – that wouldn't be true at all. But I definitely do believe that a significant portion of evangelicals are deceived into believing that you can have Jesus as your Saviour and not be permanently, radically changed. Because despite all the exceptions of wonderful, truthful preachers and teachers, I know that there are still many people that believe they can be walking down the road of life and begin to follow Jesus without having turned or changed their present path. Now this is counter intuitive. You can not turn *to* follow Christ without turning *away* from sin. Paul says,

**"Let everyone who names the name of the Lord depart from iniquity." (2 Timothy 2:19b)**

Yet so many people profess to be Christians, while continuing to walk through life as they always have. They claim to have Jesus, but are unchanged. And then the rest of the world looks at Christians in the church and they mock our gospel, saying it has no power. They scoff at Jesus because His followers are not living the life He preached about. Paul writes about people who profess to be Christians and continue living sinful lives.

**"They profess to know God, but they deny him by their works. They are detestable, disobedient, unfit for any good work. " (Titus 1:16)**

The gospel, the true gospel of Jesus, contains all truth, and is the power of God for salvation.[5] But we tend to boil it down to just the plan of

---

5    Romans 12:16

salvation. When we talk about conversions, often all we are concerned about is making sure that we're going to heaven. We seem to think that Christianity is just a way to escape hell, and we forget that it is the power of God to transform lives. I know of camps where the counsellors are instructed to pull each kid aside and make sure that they have prayed and asked Jesus to come into their heart. And if the camper hasn't, they encourage the kid to do so. But there is more to becoming a Christian than praying and asking Jesus into your heart. If all that being a Christian meant was asking Jesus into your heart and then going to heaven, the Bible would probably be only a couple pages long. There is more to having Jesus than just being saved from hell. There's more to following Jesus than going to heaven when you die.

Jesus is more than just our Saviour. He is also our Lord. One of the most repeated phrases in the gospel of Matthew is 'The Kingdom of Heaven.' You can't be part of Jesus' kingdom without having Him as your king. When Jesus teaches his disciples to pray He tells them to pray like this:

**"Your kingdom come, your will be done, on earth as it is in heaven" (Matthew 6:10).**

When a person becomes a believer - or part of the Kingdom of God - they come under the Lordship of the King of the Kingdom – who is Jesus. A.W. Tozer once said, "There is no saviourhood without Lordship. Jesus Christ is both Lord and Saviour, and He was Lord before He was Saviour, and if He's not Lord, He's not Saviour."[6] Look what John writes:

**"Whoever believes the Son has eternal life; whoever does not *obey* the Son shall not see life, but the wrath of God remains on him." (John 3:36, emphasis added.)**

Eternal life comes hand in hand with obedience. In fact, that verse is a pretty strict warning against disobedience – 'whoever does not obey

---

6    Tozer, A.W. *And He Dwelt Among Us*. Ventura, CA: Regal, 2009. Print. p. 88.

shall not see life.' This contradicts the teaching that you can continue to live however you want. I think one of the most common expressions I hear is 'Jesus will take you as you are.' And that is so true! Amen! But Jesus will not leave you as you are! Jesus has commanded all men everywhere to repent. That means to turn from your sin. And so all true believers, in coming to Christ, have turned from their sin, and Christ has changed their heart, giving them a new nature – a nature that continues to turn further from sin and draw nearer to Him. That's what we call 'growing.' Backtracking to the beginning of the verse, notice also that Jesus does not say whoever believes in the Son *will* have eternal life. He says they *have* it. Eternal life does not begin when you die. It begins the moment you believe.

**"Therefore, if anyone is in Christ, he is a new creation. The old has passed away; behold, the new has come." (2 Corinthians 5:17)**

There is no need for interpretation here. What Paul just said is that whoever is in Christ is a new creation. As in, what he is now has been newly created – it wasn't what was there before. In fact, what was there before has passed away. You can go read that verse for yourself, and the rest of 2 Corinthians 5 if you'd like (the second half of the chapter is very relevant to this discussion) – but I feel like Paul said precisely what he means. That whoever is in Christ is a new creation. A new creature. They have new life. As in, they've been born-again.

So then, let's read the negative side of that conclusion. If anyone in Christ is a new creation, therefore anyone not a new creation is not in Christ. If we are going to believe the Word of God, I think the only thing we can conclude is that if a person has not been changed, they haven't really met Christ. This verse doesn't leave any room for if-, but- or maybe-. There are no exceptions. Anyone in Christ is a new creation.

Wherever I go, and whenever I say these things, I'm always accused of being too harsh. Too stingy. 'How dare he say that if a person is unchanged they don't know Christ! You can't judge!' And you're right. I can't judge you. I can't look at you and say whether or not you are saved. But I can tell you what Jesus said:

**"Every healthy tree cannot bear bad fruit, nor can a diseased tree bear good fruit. Every tree that does not bear good fruit is cut down and thrown into the fire." (Matthew 7:18-19)**

I've heard it preached that Jesus is talking about the difference between a good Christian and a bad Christian. But the last time I checked, Christians were not described as 'diseased,' and being thrown into the fire sure doesn't sound like heaven to me. So is it wrong for us to say that if a person is unchanged – if they are bearing no fruit – they don't really know Christ? We're given new life and that life ought to produce fruit!

**"Blessed is the man who trusts in the LORD, whose trust is the LORD. He is like a tree planted by water, that sends out its roots by the stream, and does not fear when heat comes, for its leaves remain green, and is not anxious in the year of drought, for it does not cease to bear fruit." (Jeremiah 17:7-8)**

So what exactly does it mean to be given new life? What does that look like? Well, let's refresh ourselves on what we looked like before we were given new life:

**"And you were dead in the trespasses and sins in which you once walked, following the course of this world, following the prince of the power of the air, the spirit that is now at work in the sons of disobedience - among whom we all once lived in the passions of our flesh, carrying out the desires of the body and the mind, and were by nature children of wrath, like the rest of mankind." (Ephesians 2:1-3)**

So we used to be dead (spiritually) in sin. We followed Satan (that's the prince of the power of the air), who works in the sons of disobedience, who we used to all live with. And we all followed the passions of our flesh. I don't think you need to use your imagination too much to know what it means to follow sinful passions. You know full well your heart has a passion for ungodly things. Just by nature of being human there are certain wrong, sinful things that you have always had a desire for. A secret hunger for something that opposes God's spotless character. If you don't believe you've ever had a hunger for something opposing God's character, then I would say you don't really know who God is. You may think you do, but I would plead with you to get into your Bible and find out who He really is. And as you compare yourself to His spotless nature, it won't take long until you realize that even your good works are like filthy rags.[7] So we are all born with sinful passions, carrying out the desires of our body, and as such are deserving of God's wrath. But don't think everything stops there. Grab your Bible and keep reading Ephesians 2 to see how God saves us by grace, through faith.

So that is our old nature, and a little while ago we read in 2 Corinthians 5:17 that our old nature has passed away, and a new one came. Whoever is in Christ is a new creation – no longer the old follow-the-passions-of-the-flesh creature. So why do we see so many people professing Jesus as Lord and living lives that are steeped in sin?

Again, I believe it is because we have been so concerned about making sure people have prayed and asked Jesus into their heart that we have neglected the true, life-changing power of the gospel. I think, quite often we preach half of a gospel. To explain what I mean by that, let's take a moment and see exactly how Paul defines the gospel:

**"Now I would remind you brothers, of the gospel I preached to you...that Christ died for our sins in accordance with the Scriptures, that he was buried, that he was raised on the third day in accordance with the Scriptures.□" (1 Corinthians 15:1, 3-4)**

So the gospel is, quite simply, Christ's death, burial and resurrection (in accordance with the Scriptures). Again, I believe we only preach half a gospel. So often, we preach Christ crucified, but not Christ resurrected. We talk about Christ's death – how He died in our place, the perfect lamb of God, bearing our sin and shame. On the cross He bore God's wrath and justified guilty sinners. His death brings forgiveness. What glorious truth! What a marvellous message! That is the message of the cross, and the cross ought to be the centrepiece of all of our teaching. But – and here lies the problem – the gospel does not stop there. It does not stop with Jesus on the cross. Because He also rose from the dead,

---

7     Isaiah 64:6

giving new life. He trampled over death, taking away its victory and its sting,[8] defeating sin and rising as Lord and Saviour. What kind of Saviour would He be if He were left on the cross defeated by death - a result of sin – the very thing He came to conquer? No, He rose victorious and remains victorious. This is why everyone in Him is a new creation. Because you can not be in Him and continue to be defeated by what He defeated. He was victorious over sin and death and is in you – still victorious over sin and death.

**"And if Christ has not been raised, then our preaching is in vain and your faith is in vain."** (1 Corinthians 15:14)

Christ rose in new life, and He gave us new life! He didn't just save us from the ultimate penalty of sin (hell), He saved us from the presence and power of sin in our lives, here on this Earth. He forgave us, justified us, and then rose triumphant over the very thing He just forgave us of. His work would have been incomplete if He had forgiven His people and then left them in the shackles of sin. That's like pardoning a criminal but leaving him locked in the dungeon. What kind of a pardon is that?

**"And I will give you a new heart, and a new spirit I will put within you. And I will remove the heart of stone from your flesh and give you a heart of flesh. And I will put my spirit within you, and cause you to walk in my statutes and be careful to obey my rules."** (Ezekiel 36:26-27)

We are a living people. Read that verse again and see how many of those statements are promises. Notice how many times God says *I will*. Not *I might*. We are wrong to believe that you can be in Christ – be a Christian - and continue to live in the deadness of the old nature. That sin loving nature is put to death with Christ, and we are given new life in Him. You can not believe in Jesus and not be completely changed. Before we move on, you should put down this book and go read Ezekiel 37:1-14. No, seriously. Go read it.

---

[8]     1 Corinthians 15:55

Seriously. Ezekiel.

What an amazing story! It is actually my favourite Bible story. Now, Ezekiel was a prophet, and so what he saw was prophetic – it was a picture of what God was going to do in the future. First of all, it was a picture of what God was going to do to an exiled, beaten, basically dead Israel. And that's who Ezekiel speaks to first – God is going to raise dead Israel back to life, just like He raised the bones. And if you read history you'll see that that is exactly what happened. But, like most of the Old Testament, this isn't talking about just Israel, but also pointing forward to Jesus. This is a picture of what Jesus is going to do in you and in me. He's going to raise us from the spiritual dead, and breathe on us, and give us new life.

So the Christian, the person who really has Christ in their life is going to be changed. They're going to be different. When a person becomes a Christian, we often talk about 'asking Jesus in their heart.' If your heart is the very essence of who you are – the very core of your being – if it is where your thoughts and emotions come from, then just consider what it would look like to have a Holy God in there. The sin-hating, righteousness loving God in the very core of your person. Can you put the living Christ in there and have unchanged thoughts and emotions? You can not have Jesus Christ in your heart and not be permanently changed.

**"For the grace of God has appeared, bringing salvation for all people, training us to renounce ungodliness and worldly passions, and to live self-controlled, upright, and godly lives in the present age," (Titus 2:11)**

One of the best illustrations of this permanent change is by Paul Washer. "Let's imagine that I show up late and I run up here on the platform. And all the leaders are angry with me...And I say, 'brothers, you'll have to forgive me...I was out here on the highway, and I was driving, and I had a flat tire, and I got out to change the tire, and when I was changing the tire, the lugnut fell off, and I wasn't paying attention that I was on the highway, and I ran out, and I grabbed the lugnut, and soon as I picked it up in the middle of the highway, I stood up and there was a 30 tonne logging truck going 120 miles an hour about ten yards in front of me, and it ran me over, and that's why I'm late. Now, there would only be two logical conclusions...One, I'm a liar. Or two, I'm a madman. You would say, Brother Paul, it is absolutely absurd. It is impossible, Brother Paul, to have an encounter with something as large as a logging truck and not be changed. And then my question would be to you, what is larger, a logging truck, or God? How is it that so many people today profess to have had an encounter with Jesus Christ and yet they are not permanently changed? "[9]

Let me be clear with what I am saying. I *am* saying that everyone who knows Jesus has been given a new nature. They are a new creation. They have been born-again. I am *not* saying that every Christian is perfect. I am not saying that the moment a person is saved they are fully mature in their walk. I am not saying that Christians don't sin, don't face temptation, or don't fall into sinful habits again. Christians screw up. I know I've sure screwed up. And I know that's a harsh term, but I believe its appropriate to describe just how severely I have, at times, disobeyed and gone back to sin. And yet, if you were to look at my life as a whole – if you were to look at the life of any person after the moment they began to follow Jesus – you would not see sin, but victory. It was said already that eternal life doesn't begin when you die. And even though we stumble, and may turn back for a moment, we are always caught by His grace and put back on the right path.

All the time, I hear, 'Jesus loves me for who I am. He loves me, faults and all. Even when I mess up and sin, He loves me for who I am.' There's definitely some truth to that statement, but be careful to let Scripture define what Jesus' love looks like. Jesus' love does not give you the right to sin willy-nilly just because He is slow to anger and abounding in mercy. You say Jesus loves you for who you are. Jesus loves you enough to *crucify* who you are - with Him - and give you a *new* life – to redefine who you are.

**"What shall we say then? Are we to continue in sin that grace may abound? By no means! How can we who died to sin still live in it?**

---

[9] Washer, Paul. "Modern American Christianity." Sermon. Available at: http://www.sermonindex.net/modules/mydownloads/singlefile.php?lid=12827&commentView=itemComments

**Do you not know that all of us who have been baptized into Christ Jesus were baptized into His death? We were buried therefore with Him by baptism into death, in order that just as Christ was raised from the dead by the glory of the father, we too might walk in the newness of life. For if we have been united with Him in a death like His, we shall certainly be united with Him in a resurrection like His." (Romans 6:1-5)**

Everyone who is truly a believer, has been given new life. And if you are still caught in the shackles of sin – if you still love sin, and still love other things more than God, please, please, examine yourself and see if you have truly been born-again. If you are living in sin – if the things of God are still dull and boring to you, you need to know having never been remade is evidence that you have never been saved. Believe in Jesus and be changed. But please, don't take it from me. Compare yourself to the Scriptures and see for yourself. Read these verses for yourself, and ask God to examine you.

**"If we say we have fellowship with him while we walk in darkness, we lie and do not practice the truth." (1 John 1:6)**

**"Do not love the world or the things in the world. If anyone loves the world, the love of the Father is not in him." (1 John 2:15)**

**"No one born of God makes a practice of sinning, for God's seed abides in him, and he cannot keep on sinning because he has been born of God." (1 John 3:9)**

**"We know that we have passed out of death into life, because we love the brothers. Whoever does not love, abides in death." (1 John 3:14)**

**"By this we know that we love the children of God, when we love God and obey His commandments. For this is the love of God, that we keep His commandments. And His commandments are not burdensome. For everyone who has been born of God overcomes**

**the world. And this is the victory that has overcome the world – our faith.**" (1 John 5:2-4)

Do those verses describe you? Are you walking in darkness? Are you loving the things of the world? Do you love your Christian brothers (even the rude, annoying ones who don't love you back)? Do you keep His commandments, or are they burdensome to you? Do you overcome the world? Are you living the new life Christ has given us? Now, these verses are all from 1 John. And I strongly, strongly encourage you to go read the rest of the book of 1 John for yourself. Because there are plenty more verses in there that talk all about what it looks like to have Christ in you. I just picked a few. And like I said before – don't take my word for it. I am just a man. Go read the Bible yourself. Read 1 John, and ask God to show you if you are really walking in the light.

One of the central messages of the gospel is change. A giving up of the old nature, and a claiming of the new life Christ offers you. Are you walking in that new life today?

If you're not, I want to point you back to the last chapter. If you want to experience the life that Christ gives, you must experience His death. You must crawl onto that cross with Him if you want to experience His resurrection.

**"For if we have been united with him in a death like his, we shall certainly be united with him in a resurrection like his. We know that our old self was crucified with him in order that the body of sin might be brought to nothing, so that we would no longer be enslaved to sin.**" (Romans 6:5-6).

Christ has promised us new life. Have you claimed that promise as your own? Are you walking daily in victory over sin, or are you still bound by lust and pride? Is your assurance that you have been saved based on the fact that you prayed and asked Jesus to come in, or is it based on the evidence that there has been a supernatural work of God in your heart? Is your Christianity just going to church and reading your Bible, or has God really raised you from the dead to walk in Christ 24/7? Don't forget that salvation is the power of God, and God happens to be pretty powerful. Has that power been displayed in your heart?

I'm not trying to make legitimate Christians doubt their salvation. But I'd rather have real Christians thoroughly examining themselves than have false-Christians go to hell. And more than anything, I want to remind you that Christ has called you out of death into life. Christians mess up. We sin. But as a style of life, live to the glory of the Father.

**"For those who live according to the flesh set their minds on the things of the flesh, but those who live according to the Spirit set their minds on the things of the Spirit. For to set the mind on the flesh is death, but to set the mind on the Spirit is life and peace. For the mind that is set on the flesh is hostile to God, for it does not submit to God's law, indeed it cannot. Those who are in the flesh cannot please God. You, however, are not in the flesh but in the Spirit, if in fact the Spirit of God dwells in you. Anyone who does not have the Spirit of Christ does not belong to Him...If the Spirit of Him who raised Jesus from the dead lives in you, He who raised Christ Jesus from the dead will also give life to your mortal bodies through the Spirit who dwells in you." (Romans 8:5-9, 11)**

*Dear Father,*

*I see throughout Scripture of how you have taken hopeless situations and brought life.*

*I see how you breathed life into the bones in the valley when Ezekiel prophesied.*

*I see how you raised Jesus from the dead, defeating death and sin.*

*Again, I put myself on the cross, that I would be united with Christ in His death,*

*that I might be united also in His resurrection.*

*I want new life.*

*I want to walk in the new life He offers.*

*Please, grant me life according to Jesus' resurrection.*

*Seal me with your Holy Spirit, that I may walk in victory over sin.*

*In Jesus name,*

*Amen.*

## Chapter 4: Meaningless
### This chapter was co-authored with Jordan Gold

I (Kevin) remember one time I was speaking on the existence of God, and someone asked me what I'd do if I was wrong. What would I do if it were proved (somehow) beyond a shadow of a doubt that there is no God? That's easy. I'd kill myself. Why live? If there is no God, I have no purpose. None whatsoever. Without a God, this book has no purpose. Neither do your good deeds. You can feed every starving child in the world, and they may live longer, but they'll still die. If there is no God, what is the purpose of my life?

About a year ago I (Jordan) was sitting in Starbucks savouring each sip of my caramel macchiato. If there is no God in this life, and Kevin has killed himself, then caramel macchiatos are what this boy is going to live for. I was chilling with a friend that had recently abandoned ship on his former religion (a variation of the Bahá'í faith) and is now in the process of seeking another. I looked him in the eye and, straight-up man that I am, asked him: What is the purpose to your life? In the next half an hour he explained to me that the purpose to his life was to obtain ultimate freedom and joy by pleasing, at all times and at all costs, himself and by ensuring that he was always number one in his life. And isn't that where any natural human is at? Dead in sin, without the new life Christ offers, what do we live for? Freedom and joy found in pleasing ourselves. Always being number one.

In fact, the essence of sin is believing that you are number one. But if you're number one in life, than life has no purpose at all. If you're the king of your life, you are the king of a kingdom that will come to absolute ruin, because someday you are going to die.

I feel I could say more, but I want the Word of God to speak for itself. In my pride and selfishness, I want to say more – to spill out all *my* wisdom and *my* understanding. But I can't make you see truth. I can't make you want to live for God. So rather than listening to me, let's hear what God has to say through His inspired Word. Please carefully read each of these verses, and dwell on what is being said to you. If you're going to do any skimming, please let it be over our words. In the book of Ecclesiastes, we read:

**"The words of the Preacher, the son of David, king in Jerusalem.**

**Vanity of vanities, says the Preacher,
vanity of vanities! All is vanity.
What does man gain by all the toil
at which he toils under the sun?
A generation goes, and a generation comes,
but the earth remains forever.
The sun rises, and the sun goes down,
and hastens to the place where it rises.
The wind blows to the south
and goes around to the north;
around and around goes the wind,
and on its circuits the wind returns.
All streams run to the sea,
but the sea is not full;**

**to the place where the streams flow,
there they flow again." (Ecclesiastes 1:1-7)**

The word vanity really just means 'meaningless,' and after stating that everything is meaningless in the first verse, I think he does a really good job of proving that. Its meaningless. Look at nature! Whatever happens, ends up 'unhappening.' The rivers go to all that work (figuratively speaking) of trying to fill the sea, but the sea never fills up! It is pointless.

**"All things are full of weariness;
a man cannot utter it;
the eye is not satisfied with seeing,
nor the ear filled with hearing.
What has been is what will be,
and what has been done is what will be done,
and there is nothing new under the sun.**

**Is there a thing of which it is said,**

**"See, this is new?"**

**It has been already**

**in the ages before us." (Ecclesiastes 1:8-10)**

Well that's discouraging. But its true. Your eyes are never satisfied. Neither are your ears. They've always got to be re-filled. And it certainly does a good job of taking us off our high horse and putting us back where we belong. I feel like what's being said to me is, 'really? You think you're so smart? Someone has already thought it. You think you're accomplishing something great? That's been done too. You think what you're living for is fantastic? Wrong.' Makes you a little less impressed with yourself, doesn't it?

**"It is an unhappy business that God has given the children of man to be busy with. I have seen everything that is done under the sun, and behold, all is vanity and a striving after the wind." (Ecclesiastes 1:13b-14)**

Rather depressing isn't it? The Bible says life is like chasing after the wind. We're all busy with something that has been done before. And we're all deceived into thinking that we'll find purpose in these things. Running around and around, and accomplishing nothing. But does that make life meaningless? The author (who is probably Solomon) started off by saying *everything* is meaningless. But just because its been done before doesn't mean its meaningless, right? You can find meaning in the things you do, can't you? Let's see what Solomon says.

**"I said in my heart, "Come now, I will test you with pleasure; enjoy yourself." But behold, this also was vanity. I said of laughter, "It is mad," and of pleasure, "What use is it?" I searched with my heart how to cheer my body with wine—my heart still guiding me with wisdom—and how to lay hold on folly, till I might see what was good for the children of man to do under heaven during the few days of their life. I made great works. I built houses and planted vineyards for myself. I made myself gardens and parks, and planted in them all kinds of fruit trees. I made myself pools from which to water the forest of growing trees. I bought male and female slaves, and had slaves who were born in my house. I had also great possessions of herds and flocks, more than any who had been before me in Jerusalem. I also gathered for myself silver and gold and the treasure of kings and provinces. I got singers, both men and women, and many concubines, the delight of the sons of man.**

**So I became great and surpassed all who were before me in Jerusalem. Also my wisdom remained with me. And whatever my eyes desired I did not keep from them. I kept my heart from no pleasure, for my heart found pleasure in all my toil, and this was**

**my reward for all my toil. Then I considered all that my hands had done and the toil I had expended in doing it, and behold, all was vanity and a striving after wind, and there was nothing to be gained under the sun." (Ecclesiastes 2:1-11)**

When we look at history, we find that the man writing this was one of the wealthiest kings that has ever lived. So let's just be clear – this guy had it made. Everything you want, he had. Nothing held him back. And what did he find? Pleasure, yes. But meaning? No.

Laughter. Pleasure. Great works. Riches. Concubines (sex). Greatness. Anything he wanted. Anything that gave him pleasure

Meaningless.

All of it.

**"Then I said in my heart, what happens to the fool will happen to me also. 'Why then, have I been so very wise?' And I said in my heart that this also is vanity." (Ecclesiastes 2:15)**

**"So I turned about and gave my heart up to despair over all the toil of my labours under the sun, because sometimes a person who has toiled with wisdom and knowledge and skill must leave everything to be enjoyed by someone who did not toil for it. This also is vanity and a great evil." (Ecclesiastes 2:20-21)**

What are you working for? What are you living for? Don't you see? Its all meaningless! You work and work and strive and strive, and you find a nice spouse and live in a nice house and have a nice car. And you can even live a nice Christian life, and be wise and hardworking. And you'll still die. Just like all the poor, lazy people who didn't accomplish any of the things you did.

If there is no God - why live?
If there is nothing beyond this life, nothing beyond what you accomplish here on Earth, there is no purpose.
Why seek pleasure?

Why seek to be wise?
Why seek to be Godly?
Why work?
Why live?
Why not just go drink caramel macchiatos forever?

**"For what happens to the children of man and what happens to the beasts is the same; as one dies, so dies the other. They all have the same breath, and man has no advantage over the beasts, for all is vanity. All go to one place. All are from the dust, and to the dust all return." (Ecclesiastes 3:19-20)**

We're just skipping through Ecclesiastes – picking out some key verses. You should actually just go and read the whole book for yourself. But we think the message should be super clear – life is absolutely meaningless. Unless - and that's a pretty big unless – unless there is a God. See, so far the author has been saying that 'everything under the sun' is meaningless. But just so that we understand Hebrew poetry here - 'under the sun' is referring to a picture that has taken God out of the equation. Take God out of life and it is all pointless.

The only meaning you'll ever find in life is in fellowship with Christ. That is it. Everything, literally everything else in all creation will leave you feeling more and more empty. Just like trying to digest air, it doesn't matter how much you take in for food: you will still feel hungry, and the more you chase after air to quench your hunger, the hungrier you shall become.

**"He who loves money will not be satisfied with money, nor he who loves wealth with his income; this also is vanity." (Ecclesiastes 5:10)**

So then, the only thing that matters in life is your response to Christ.

Is He where you find satisfaction? Is He at the centre point of your life? Or are you filled with pride? What do you concern yourself with? With finding pleasure for *yourself*? With making a name for *yourself*? Who is at the centre of all that you do? You, or God? Because, everything that is not built upon God will pass away.

"As he comes from his mother's womb he shall go again, naked as he came, and shall take nothing for his toil that he may carry away in his hand." (Ecclesiastes 5:15)

How you respond to God is of the utmost importance, because everything in life revolves not around you, but around Him. What you will do has already been done before, and will end anyways. The only thing that will last, is the pursuit of the eternal. God has no end, so what you build upon Him will not perish with the rest of the world.

"Guard your steps when you go to the house of God. To draw near to listen is better than to offer the sacrifice of fools, for they do not know that they are doing evil. Be not rash with your mouth, nor let your heart be hasty to utter a word before God, for God is in heaven and you are on Earth. Therefore let your words be few." (Ecclesiastes 5:1-2)

The pursuit of anything (including righteousness) that is not God is like chasing after the wind.

"...just as he came, so shall he go, and what gain is there to him who toils for the wind?" (Ecclesiastes 5:16)

"All the toil of man is for his mouth, yet his appetite is not satisfied." (Ecclesiastes 6:7)

"But all this I laid to heart, examining it all, how the righteous and the wise and their deeds are in the hand of God. Whether it is love or hate, man does not know; both are before him. It is the same for all, since the same event happens to the righteous and the wicked, to the good and the evil, to the clean and the unclean, to him who sacrifices and him who does not sacrifice. As the good one is, so is the sinner, and he who swears is as he who shuns an oath. This is an evil in all that is done under the sun, that the same event happens to all. Also the hearts of the children of man are full of evil, and madness is in their hearts while they live, and after that they go to the dead. But he who is joined with all the living has hope, for a living dog is better than a dead lion. For the living know

**that they will die, but the dead know nothing, and they have no more reward, for the memory of them is forgotten. Their love, and their hate, and their envy have already perished, and forever they have no more share in all that is done under the sun." (Ecclesiastes 9:1-6)**

Even in the church, there are a lot of purposes that we will strenuously reach for that turn out. We will pump our church full of attenders until we need a new building (and then move and build a bigger one and then continue this process) or any other unattainable goal that there really is no end to. This is the apex of what human nature teaches us: acquire as much as you possibly can. But can't we see that at the very centre of our being lies something that is completely and totally empty? Solomon had *everything* and yet teaches that even when he had everything, he realized it was all useless.

**"Remember also your Creator in the days of your youth, before the evil days will say "I have no pleasure in them." (Ecclesiastes 12:1)**

And so Solomon studied all things, and with his great wisdom, examined all of life. And here is the conclusion he came to.

**"The end of the matter, all has been heard. Fear God and keep His commandments, for this is the whole duty of man. For God will bring every deed into judgement, with every secret thing, whether good or evil." (Ecclesiastes 12:13-14)**

*Dear Father,*
*The purpose of life is to serve you and keep your commandments.*
*Everything else is meaningless.*
*God, help me to live for you and you alone.*
*God, may I live not for myself, but for the things that have eternal value.*
*May every purpose in my life be derived from you.*
*May fellowship with you be the only thing in life I seek.*
*In Jesus name,*
*Amen.*

## Chapter 5: You Don't Have it, Because You Don't Want it

If you love somebody, you want to know them. God loves you. In fact, God is love. Its part of His very character. That's probably a very familiar concept to you. We write 'Jesus loves you' on bumper stickers and erasers and write it in Sharpie on the walls of our youth rooms. Jesus loves you. But do you love Jesus? Do you really want to know Him? Do you want to draw near to Him, and talk with Him, and learn from Him? Do you want Him to shape your life, do you want Him to *be* your life, or do you just want Him to be a part of it? Do you just want to hear Bible stories about Jesus or do you want to know Jesus on a personal, intimate level? Because knowing who somebody is and *knowing* them are two very different things. Do you want to *know Jesus* on a personal level, or are you satisfied to read your Bible and *know who Jesus is*?

Now I'm writing this to Christians. I'm not talking about the difference between knowing Jesus is able to save and knowing Him as your Saviour. There are a lot of non-Christians who know who Jesus is but don't know Him personally. I'm not talking about that. No, I'm writing this to those of you that are already believers. Who know Him as your Lord and Saviour. You can know all about Jesus. What He said, how He acted, what He did. You can know Him as your personal Saviour - and then you can *know* Him on a real and intimate level.

When we talk about the will of God, we are often concerned about what we must do and where we must go. That's the big question for folks graduating from high school. What is God's will for my life now? Where does He want me? But as I read the Scriptures, I see a God who is more concerned about the *who* than the *where*. He cares more about relationship than work. The country of Israel wandered around in the desert for forty years because God cared more about who they were than where He wanted them. They were rebellious and idolatrous – so He gave them law, gave them a tabernacle and let a whole generation die, so He could shape them into *who* He wanted them to be. Then when He was done working on the who, He brought into the *where* – the Promised Land.

Sometimes we spend so much time seeking the *will* of God we forget to seek *God*. God wants to be known by you. Henry Blackaby writes, "I think God is often crying out and shouting to us, 'Don't just do something. Stand there! Enter into a love relationship with Me. Get to know Me. Adjust your life to Me. Let Me love you and reveal myself to you as I work through you.' A time will come when the doing is called for, but we cannot skip the relationship. The relationship with God must come first."[10]

This chapter is all about *knowing* God. You can know who God is, and understand His character, and His plans, and His nature, and His gospel, and His word, and His son. But there is a far higher level of intimacy available to the believer. You can know Him, and you can *know* Him.

You can know Him – be a Christian, and you can *know* Him – have intimacy.

The easiest way to explain this difference is by studying the presence of God. Hopefully this will help to make the difference between knowing and *knowing* more clear. God is omnipresent. That means He is absolutely everywhere at once. He is sitting on both sides of you. Anywhere you could possibly go, He is there, because He isn't a God who is just 'big' but a God who far exceeds our understanding. Right now He is as near to you as He could possibly be. I am writing this at a different time, and in a different place than where you are and yet I know God is right here beside me, and right there beside you. He is everywhere.

> "Where shall I go from your Spirit?
> Or where shall I flee from your presence?
> If I ascend to heaven, you are there!
> If I make my bed in Sheol, you are there! (Psalm 139:7-8)

He is omnipresent. If that information is boring and old to you, and doesn't cause you to stand in awe and adore Him, it is because you know Him, but don't *know* Him. You know God is omnipresent, but you aren't beholding His glory. God is so majestic that when we even glimpse His glory, it ought to put us on our faces in awe and reverence.

---

10   Blackaby, Henry. *Experiencing God*. Nashville, TN: Broadman & Holman Publisjers, 1998. Print. p. 30.

So God is omnipresent. But there is also the *manifest* presence of God. There are times and places when God *comes*, even though He is already everywhere. Let's look at what happened at the inauguration of the tabernacle.

**"Then the cloud covered the tent of meeting, and the glory of the LORD filled the tabernacle. And Moses was not able to enter the tent of meeting because the cloud settled on it, and the glory of the LORD filled the tabernacle." (Exodus 40:34-35)**

There are several instances throughout Scripture where God manifests His presence. Some of the most famous instances would be on Mt. Sinai, Mt. Carmel or at Pentecost. God has always been omnipresent, and was still omnipresent, yet in these instances He manifested something *more* of His glory, something *more* of His power, something *more* of His presence. The God who was as near as He could be drew nearer still. This is why throughout the Old Testament, God threatens to remove His presence from Israel, or remove Israel from His presence. He wouldn't stop being everywhere, but He would remove His *manifest* presence.

And this is the difference between knowing God and *knowing* God. God can be near to you (He already is), and God can be *near* to you. He is omnipresent, but He can be manifest. Do you *know* Him? Do you, as an individual experience God, or is He just a concept to you? Do you really *know* Him? Do you know Him in the sense that He is near (omnipresent) to you, or do you know Him in the sense that He is near (manifest) to you?

Because God *can* be manifest in your life. That is the promise to every believer. God's presence used to be manifest in the Holy of Holies in the temple, but at Christ's death, the curtain to the Holy of Holies tore, because that manifest Presence is no longer confined to the temple (but more on that in chapter 7). He is ready and willing to come and fill the heart of the Christian.

**"What father among you, if his son asks for a fish, will instead of a fish give him a serpent; or if he asks for an egg, will give him a**

**scorpion? If you then, who are evil, know how to give good gifts to your children, how much more will the heavenly Father give the Holy Spirit to those who ask him!" (John 7:38)**

**"To each is given the manifestation of the Spirit for the common good." (1 Corinthians 12:7)**

You must know that this promise is for you and claim it as your own. This is God's promise to you. Faith is always the foundation for any relationship with God, so before we go anywhere, you need to know that unless you *believe* God's promises for you, you can never have them.

Do you long to be with Him? Does your soul ache to be met by the Living God? Do you hunger and thirst for Him? Is He the longing of your heart, the centrepiece of your affections, the highest yearning of your soul?

Because when I read the Bible, I don't see men and women who were indifferent towards their relationship with God. I don't see men and women who were satisfied to be saved by grace and then live their days with a biblical knowledge of the Holy. I see men and women who were on their faces with broken hearts pleading for more of God. Jacob wrestled with God all night long and refused to let Him go until He blessed him (Genesis 33:26). Moses lay prostrate on his face for forty days and forty nights interceding for the Israelites (Deuteronomy 9:25). Hannah was so deeply distressed she wept bitterly and prayed without using words until the priest thought she was drunk (1 Samuel 1:10, 13).

Does your heart ache and cry and long for the Lord? Or have you experienced His goodness, experienced His grace and remained unmoved in response?

David Brainerd was a missionary to the Natives in New Hampshire in the late 1700s. Daily, he wrote of how he would wrestle with God in prayer. Brainerd was not satisfied to kneel by his bed and speak to God. He wanted to know all that God had for him. He wanted to truly know the Lord in prayer. Here is an excerpt from his diary.

"Felt somewhat of the sweetness of communion with God, and the constraining force of his love; how admirably it captivates the soul, and makes all the desires and affections centre in God! - I set apart this day for secret fasting and prayer, to entreat God to direct and bless me with regard to the great work which I have in view, of preaching the gospel - and that the Lord would return to me, and individually "show me the light of his countenance." Had little life and power in the forenoon: near the middle of the afternoon God enabled me to wrestle ardently in intercession for absent friends: but just at night the Lord visited me marvellously in prayer. I think my soul never was in such an agony before. I felt no restraint, for the treasures of divine grace were opened to me. I wrestled for absent friends, for the ingathering of souls, for multitudes of poor souls, and for many that I thought were the children of God, in many distant places. I was in such an agony, for half an hour before sunset, till near dark, that I was all over wet with sweat: but yet is seemed to me that I had wasted away the day, and had done nothing. Oh!, my dear Saviour did sweat blood for poor souls! I longed for more compassion toward them."[11]

Do you *know* Him in prayer? Do you set apart days for secret fasting and prayer like Brainerd, because your heart longs for God? Do you have little life and power in the forenoon and give up? Do you wrestle in prayer, or do you just talk? Do you *know* Him?

And more importantly - do you *want* to *know* Him? You won't *know* Him if you don't want him. You can't claim His promise if you don't want to claim His promise. For God will satisfy you to exactly the level you thirst to.

**"Blessed are those who hunger and thirst for righteousness, for they shall be satisfied." (Matthew 5:6)**

Christ has promised that if you thirst for righteousness, you *will* be satisfied. Quite often the reason we don't have more of God is because we don't want any more of Him. We pray for God to bring our friends and loved ones to Him. We want Him to give them new life, but we don't pray for new life with desperation like Rachel did – "Give me

---

[11]  Edwards, Jonathan. *The Life and Diary of David Brainerd.*, Public Domain. June 14 entry.

children or I shall die!" (Genesis 30:1) Perhaps the reason you don't have or know God is because you don't really want Him. You can say you want Him, but if you're desire doesn't produce action, is that truly a desire? If you say you want God, but don't take any time to seek Him – to pour over the Scriptures, to pray and fast – how great is that desire? Do you want to *know* God? Is your thirsting for God so great that it produces action?

Here are some promises that God gave Israel:

**"But from there you will seek the Lord your God and you will find Him, if you search after Him with all your heart and with all your soul." (Deuteronomy 4:29)**

**"You will seek me and find me, when you seek me with all your heart." (Jeremiah 29:13)**

And then here are Jesus' words to us:

**"Ask, and it will be given to you; seek, and you will find; knock, and it will be opened to you. For everyone who asks receives, and the one who seeks finds, and to the one who knocks it will be opened." (Matthew 7:7-8)**

God is not hiding from you. If you want God, God will be found by you. In fact, God wants to be found by you. But I fear many Christians do not desire Him enough to seek Him. They live in His omnipresence, surrounded by Him on all sides, but never have any thirst for His manifest presence. They are satisfied with a mediocre love relationship with the God of the universe. But my heart desires to cry with the Psalmist:

**My soul longs, yes, faints for the courts of the Lord. (Psalm 84:2a)**

I don't know about you, but I hunger to hunger, and I thirst to thirst. I want to want God, and I desire to meet with Him. I want to know Him more intimately, and most days I wish I hungered more than I really do. Not just because I might get anything out of it – but because I love

Him. Does your soul long for God? Do you desire to draw nearer to Him? I think some of the Psalms really capture that desperate soul-cry to just know the Lord. When I read the Psalms, I can almost hear the Psalmists' hearts just crying in agony to know the Lord. Please read these these Psalms very carefully, and as you read, pray along with the writer.

> "Give ear to my words, O LORD;
> consider my groaning.
> Give attention to the sound of my cry,
> my King and my God,
> for to you do I pray.
>
> But I, through the abundance of your steadfast love,
> will enter your house.
> I will bow down toward your holy temple
> in the fear of you." (Psalm 5:1, 7)

> "As a deer pants for flowing streams,
> so pants my soul for you, O God.
> My soul thirsts for God,
> for the living God.
> When shall I come and appear before God?
> My tears have been my food
> day and night," (Psalm 42:1-3)

> O God, you are my God; earnestly I seek you;
> my soul thirsts for you;
> my flesh faints for you,
> as in a dry and weary land where there is no water.
> So I have looked upon you in the sanctuary,
> beholding your power and glory.
> Because your steadfast love is better than life,
> my lips will praise you. (Psalm 63:1-2)

Take a few moments and meditate on those Psalms. Talk to God about them, and tell Him where you're at. If you know you aren't really thirsty for Him, but want to be – tell Him that. If the reason you don't know

God on an intimate level is because you don't really have any desire for that, talk to Him about it as you reread those Psalms.

*Oh God, we thirst for you. We thirst to thirst more. Forgive our indifference.*

**Will you not revive us again that your people may rejoice in you? (Psalm 85:6)**

As David Brainerd pursued God, he wrote this:

"But of late, God has been pleased to keep my soul hungry, almost continually, so I have been filled with kind of a pleasing pain. When I really enjoy God, I feel my desires of Him the more insatiable, and my thirsting after holiness the more unquenchable. And the Lord will not allow me to feel as though I were fully supplied and satisfied, but keeps me still reaching forward...Oh for holiness! Oh, for more of God in my soul! Oh, this pleasing pain! It makes my soul press hard after God"[12]

Brainerd had tuberculosis. For many long years he was bent double, coughing up blood and mucus. In the days before antibiotics, he would have constantly been in excruciating pain. While weak, and slowly, slowly dying, Brainerd's passion for his Saviour never died. Suffering was no excuse to neglect his prayer duties. He spent long hours in prayer, not to ask for healing, but to ask for more of God. More of God in his own life. More of God in the hearts of those he was preaching to. He passed away in the home of Jonathan Edwards when he was 29, and is now spending eternity with the God he spent his short, hard life seeking.

Do you know God? Do you want Him? Do you want to know and experience the fulness of the Presence of God in your life? Because if you would be more content reading about God than experiencing Him, you'll never experience Him. If you're content to know of Him but not *know* Him, you will never *know* Him. Indifference is killing us.

---

12    Edwards, Jonathan. *The Life and Diary of David Brainerd.*, Public Domain. Thursday, November 4 entry.

"I want the presence of God Himself, or I don't want anything at all to do with religion... I want all that God has or I don't want any." - A.W. Tozer[13]

*Dear Father,*
*I hunger and thirst for you.*
*I don't want to live an average, ordinary life apart from Your fullness.*
*I want you. I want all of you.*
*I want to want you more.*
*I am thirsty, and pray you would reveal yourself to me that I might be thirstier still.*
*Here I am in my pursuit of you,*
*reveal yourself to me I pray.*
*I am desperate for your touch.*
*In Jesus name,*
*Amen.*

---

[13] Tozer, A.W. "Who is the Holy Spirit?" Sermon. Available at: http://www.sermonaudio.com/sermoninfo.asp?SID=9280215524

# Chapter 6: You Want Me to Look Like What?!

At one point, the question in the front of my mind was, how do I live a Christian life in high school? I can still clearly remember how much pornography was kicking around the classrooms during silent reading and how foul language became so normal I stopped noticing it. I remember my friends going to watch movies that, as a Christian, I did not want to see, and how hard it was to stay at home by myself – not even because I cared about the movie, but sometimes just because I wanted to hang out with my friends. It's still pretty fresh in my mind, that living the life God has called us to in high school is tough. And something I've discovered – it doesn't get easier. I'm done high school, but at the place I worked this spring there were still dirty posters hanging in the staff room around the table where my coworkers sat and talked about filthy sexual things. There is still sin, crouching around every corner, waiting to snare us.

**"Therefore, preparing your minds for action, and being sober-minded, set your hope fully on the grace that will be brought to you at the revelation of Jesus Christ. As obedient children, do not be conformed to the passions of your former ignorance, but as he who called you is holy, you also be holy in all your conduct, since it is written, "You shall be holy, for I am holy." (1 Peter 1:13-16)**

What is holiness? Well, quite simply, it is cleanliness, or purity. It means not having a spot or speck of anything dirty or unclean on you. Some people would also add that it means to be set apart. I would accept that definition as long as we clarify that it means to be set apart from that which is unclean, or impure – something that is holy is something that is completely set apart from things that might defile.

When Isaiah was swept up into God's throne room, there were seraphim flying around the Lord crying, 'Holy, holy, holy.[14]' About 800 years later, the apostle John was sitting on the isle of Patmos, when he too was swept up to heaven. He also saw some creatures around God's throne, and what were they singing? 'Holy, holy, holy.[15]' After 800

---

14   Isaiah 6:3

15   Revelation 4:8

years, they were still singing the same song in heaven (and I don't doubt they are still singing that same song today). Typically if my iPod gets left on repeat, I get pretty eager to change the song. Or if I go to a worship service and we end up singing one of those choruses with words that don't really make sense 12 times in a row, I get kind of bored. So there must be some pretty serious significance to 'holy, holy, holy.' They don't sing 'omnipotent, omnipotent, omnipotent,' or 'love, love, love.' But they sing 'holy, holy, holy.' God is holy. He is pure. He is clean. He is undefiled by any sin or evil. He is untouched by any vile thing, and this is recognized as the part of His character that is worthy of the most recognition. And because holiness is such an important part of God's character, in Leviticus He had commanded His people to be exactly the same.

**"For I am the LORD your God. Consecrate yourselves therefore, and be holy, for I am holy. You shall not defile yourselves with any swarming thing that crawls on the ground." (Leviticus 11:44)**

**"Speak to all the congregation of the people of Israel and say to them, You shall be holy, for I the LORD your God am holy." (Leviticus 19:2)**

**"Consecrate yourselves, therefore, and be holy, for I am the LORD your God." (Leviticus 20:7)**

God is pure and spotless, and He expects His people to be the same. He had rescued Israel out of Egypt, and it was not going to be acceptable for them to go back to the idols and the practices of the country He had just saved them from. So He gave them the law, outlining just how they were to be pure – how they were to value mercy, and abstain from impure sexual relations, and recognize that in God they were lacking nothing. Kevin DeYoung writes this,

"There's no question that holiness is one of the central themes in the Bible. The word 'holy' occurs more than 600 times in the Bible, more than 700 when you include derivative words like holiness, sanctify, and sanctification. You can't make sense of the Bible without understanding that God is holy and that this holy God is intent on making a holy people (the priests) with holy clothes in a holy land (Canaan), at a holy place (tabernacle/temple), using holy utensils and holy objects, celebrating holy days, living by a holy law, so that they might be a kingdom of priests and a holy nation."16

But don't think that the holiness commanded in the Old Testament was for the Israelites alone. God's expectation for His people has not changed. He wasn't going to let Israel wander back to the idolatrous land He had just saved them from (and besides, he had just crushed most of those folks in the Red Sea) and He isn't about to let you wander back either. In Scripture, where there is a passage on the mercy and salvation of God, it is often followed by a call to action or to holiness. He saves us, and then, in light of His mercies, implores us to no longer have anything to do with the sin He has saved us from.

**"For...you were at one time disobedient to God but now have *received mercy*...Oh, the depth of the riches and wisdom and knowledge of God!...How unsearchable are his judgements and how inscrutable his ways!...I appeal to you therefore, brothers, by the mercies of God, to *present your bodies as a living sacrifice, holy and acceptable to God*, which is your spiritual worship. *Do not be conformed to this world*, but be transformed by the renewal of your mind, that by testing you may discern what is the will of God, what is good and acceptable and perfect." (Romans11:30a, 33, 12:1-2, emphasis added)**

**Therefore do not be ashamed of the testimony about our Lord...who *saved us* and *called us to a holy calling*, not because of our works but because of his own purpose and grace, which he gave us in Christ Jesus before the ages began (2 Timothy 1:8a, 9, emphasis added)**

**For the grace of God has appeared, *bringing salvation* for all people, *training us to renounce ungodliness and worldly passions*, and to live self-controlled, upright, and godly lives in the present age (Titus 2:11-12, emphasis added)**

16    DeYoung, Kevin. *The Hole in Our Holiness.* Wheaton, IL: Crossway, 2012. Print., p. 31

**Beloved, I urge you as sojourners and exiles to *abstain from the passions of the flesh*, which wage war against your soul. Keep your conduct among the Gentiles honourable, so that when they speak against you as evildoers, they may see your good deeds and glorify God on the day of visitation. (1 Peter 2:11-12, emphasis added)**

When He saved you from the punishment of sin, He saved you from the passion you had for that sin. He saved you so you could live a pure life, one that no longer has anything to do with all those things your heart used to look to.

**Since therefore Christ suffered in the flesh, arm yourselves with the same way of thinking, for whoever has suffered in the flesh has ceased from sin, so as to live for the rest of the time in the flesh no longer for human passions but for the will of God. For the time that is past suffices for doing what the Gentiles want to do, living in sensuality, passions, drunkenness, orgies, drinking parties, and lawless idolatry. (1 Peter 4:1-3)**

Now hold on. I know what you're thinking. We all make mistakes. We're human, and God doesn't expect us to be perfect. If we were perfect, no one ever would have invented those little erasers that go on the ends of pencils. But the truth is that if you're going to ever get into heaven, God does expect you to be perfect. In Revelation, while speaking of God dwelling with man in the New Jerusalem, He says this,

**"The one who conquers will have this heritage, and I will be his God and he will be my son. But as for the cowardly, the faithless, the detestable, as for murderers, the sexually immoral, sorcerers, idolaters, and all liars, their portion will be in the lake that burns with fire and sulfur, which is the second death." (Revelation 21:7-8)**

However, by grace, Jesus Christ lived the perfect life you weren't able to live so that through His perfection, you can get to God. So when God says that this heritage is given to the one who conquers, you need to understand that Jesus is the ultimate conqueror. He lived the perfectly holy life, free from all the immoral things that are named in that passage. And then He called us to be holy like He is. So He has already conquered for us, and then tells us to also conquer. For this reason, explaining how to be holy like He is holy is kind of complicated (partly because I don't have any definitive formula for holiness, and partly because your holiness is somewhat of a paradox). It would take me an entire book to even begin to properly examine the issue of holiness, but I'll try to highlight a few key areas here in as short a space as possible. So, just so that you don't get too overwhelmed, let me give you an outline of how we're going to approach this, and hopefully it will provide you with some clarity as we try to concisely, and yet thoroughly, examine how to be holy as God is holy.

Outline:
    1. Dealing with failure that makes us unholy
    2. Recognizing unity with Christ makes us completely holy
    3. Examining the part we play in the process of becoming holy

**1. Dealing with failure that makes us unholy**

One of the most discouraging and disappointing things we face in Christianity is our own lack of holiness. This point doesn't really deal with the question of how to be holy, but I couldn't talk about holiness without taking the time to deal with failure. Those days come when temptation rises up, and we fall. We let sin have its way in our life for a time, and we feel so defeated. There is guilt and shame – sometimes self-hatred which can even lead to self-harm. I have more than one Christian friend that, after a pornography binge, has thrown themselves onto railroad tracks, or just screamed at the sky for God to kill them if He wants to. They're just ready to be crushed by the Almighty.

Sin makes us feel inadequate. We often become convinced that God can't love us anymore, or, at the least, that He can't use us anymore. When we sin, it distorts our view of God's character. We believe in a God whose love ceases, or a God who is quick to anger and short on mercy. In short, we mess up and we hate ourselves for it. We fail and we feel like failures, because God called us to be holy, and we aren't being holy.

In the last chapter we talked about pursuing God – about desiring Him. But some days it sure feels as though we have fallen out of that pursuit. For a time you wanted God, but then you made a wrong choice and demonstrated that you wanted sin more. It feels as if that burning, hungering, spirit-filled life is just out of reach. You think to yourself that there is just no way you could ever live like Paul, with his heart sold out for the gospel, because somewhere deep inside your heart there is idolatry, or a shackle of sin that still lingers. Or even though you want to be living a life that radiates with Jesus, you're so proud, and so prone to gossip you feel you could never rise to a place of godliness where people will look at you and see Christ. You feel you lack that perfection that is needed to really pursue God. Everywhere I go I meet Christians struggling with depression and self-harm. And quite often those issues started because of guilt from sin. Setbacks in sanctification were crushing.

Other times I meet people steeped in law so they can avoid the sin that so easily entangles them. I was working at a camp once, where the girls had to go to the swimming pool with a t-shirt on and the genders sat on opposite sides of the chapel. It wasn't a legalistic camp, but you could hardly say we were being promiscuous. Still, we got an angry phone call from a parent before his kid arrived. Too much association with girls - he wanted a boys-only camp. I don't know the man, but I'm using my imagination and guessing he understood and experienced some of the struggles of being a teenage boy with a growing sexual appetite. He was trying to keep his son from stumbling. Sometimes we are like him, too. We try to manage sin by making more and more rules. We know it's wrong, so we rearrange our lives until we can't fall back into it. We want nothing to taint our process of becoming more like Christ. We do not want to stumble into sin for fear it would keep us from having a life that could be used by God.

God is always making us holy, but when we stumble from that path, it is so discouraging. We hate failure and often rather than finding victory over sin we just rearrange our lives so we don't have to deal with sin. Whether it's by punishing yourself or making changes in your life to avoid anything that could be tempting, we try on our own to grow into greater holiness, and then when we fall we let ourselves down.

The truth is that wherever there is progress, there will always be failure. One time, the Israelites were living in exile in Babylon when King Cyrus let the Israelites go back to Jerusalem to rebuild the temple.[17] There seemed to be tremendous progress for a while, as God's defeated people finally returned to the Promised Land and began to restore the temple. But it wasn't long before they ended up being forcibly stopped by a group of men who didn't like Jerusalem's history.[18] But God is good. He had been in the process of reviving His nation, and His work will not be stopped. Under the prophet Haggai, Zerubabel and some others started up the work again.[19] As they worked there were more challenges, but eventually they did complete the temple.

That's the way it always is. God is building your life. God is working in you. And then there is a setback – you've gone two steps forward and you stumble a step back. God is still good. The work begins again. I don't doubt the Israelites felt they had fallen too far for God to still care about them. They had been beaten and carried off, and their cities burned and turned to rubble. But the truth is that God is far too worthy to not be willing to glorify Himself in someone's life. Israel had been defeated because of their disobedience, but God was still worthy of their praise, and so He would restore them. Countless times throughout the Old Testament God promised that if they came back to Him, He would come back to them.

And that's the way it is with you and me. God is way too worthy to stop being glorified by your life – failures and all. Because He is worthy of your praise, He will always be willing to renew in you a heart that is able to praise. He will never give up on you. And the reason for that is simple – His hope was never in you. He was never relying on you to be perfect. In fact, the only thing you contribute to salvation is sin. It's the work of the Son that will save you and make you blameless. The Father loves the Son, and the Son is in you. The Son is perfect, and so when God looks at you (even the night after you've fallen into temptation) He sees His pure, blameless Son. The holiness that you need, is found not

---

17      Ezra 1:1

18      Ezra 4:6-24

19      Ezra 5:1-2

in anything you can do, or refrain from doing, it is found in a Person, and that Person is Jesus. This leads us to our second point.

## 2. Recognizing Unity with Christ Makes us Completely Holy

When you believe in Christ, you become one with Him. When a man and a woman get married, they become one flesh. Although they are still individual people, spiritually they become one person when they unite physically. That is how it is between Jesus and believers. When you believe in Him, you become one with Him (not physically, but spiritually). In the Bible, Jesus is referred to as the bridegroom and the church is referred to as the bride. Jesus and the church will be unified spiritually, just like a husband and wife are unified physically. You, as a Christian, have been made one with Christ.

That's why you will be able to go to heaven. Because despite your sin, Christ is still blameless, and He is in you and you are in Him. No matter how much you sin, you can't make Jesus any less perfect. The Father will never stop loving the Son, and so as long as you are in Christ and Christ is in you, He will not stop loving you. No matter how badly you mess up, Jesus, the Son of God, is still able to walk into the Presence of God Almighty without shame. And because you are one with Him, you can do the same, despite all your failures. Because Jesus, in His righteousness, has the access to God that we have fallen short of.

**There is therefore now no condemnation for those who are in Christ Jesus. For the law of the Spirit of life has set you free in Christ Jesus from the law of sin and death. (Romans 8:1-2)**

Being set apart from the world is not achieved by avoiding all the things that are hip and cool. It isn't found by naming all the things that are closely associated with a secular society and avoiding them. You won't be holy because you do certain things or don't hang out with certain people. Holiness is not a set of rules to follow, it is a person – the one who kept every rule God ever made. His perfection is yours. How can you be holy? In short, you are. He is, and consequentially, you are.

Don't misunderstand me, I'm not trying to misplace repentance. I'm not suggesting you don't need to deal with your sin. If you think that unity with Christ gives you license to sin freely, you are a fool, and you need to go back and reread your Bible. In fact, it's quite the opposite, because when you sin, you are sinning against the body of Christ. Whenever you deface your own eyes, or mind or body, you are defacing Christ. This is why Paul warns the Corinthians against sexual immorality,

**"Do you not know that your bodies are members of Christ Himself? Shall I then take the members of Christ and unite them with a prostitute? Never!" (1 Corinthians 6:15)**

When non-Christian sin, they do what they know. But when believers sin, they sin against knowledge, grace, light, and against something that was made in the very image of God.[20]

**"For certain people have crept in unnoticed who long ago were designated for this condemnation, ungodly people, who pervert the grace of our God into sensuality and deny our only Master and Lord, Jesus Christ." (Jude 4)**

Don't let grace water down the definition of sin – God is love, but when you sin, you are spurning that love. That is why there is condemnation for these men – the greater the love you spurn, the greater the wrath. I don't want to make light of sin, but I do want you to understand, that no matter how heinous your sin is, Jesus is still holy, and He still stands on your behalf. When we do sin, we have someone who is blameless that we hide in. He speaks on our behalf, the way a husband speaks on behalf of his wife.

**"My little children, I am writing these things to you so that you may not sin. But if anyone does sin, we have an advocate with the Father, Jesus Christ the righteous." (1 John 2:1)**

---

20  See Greening, Mark. "Revival Now" Sermon. Available at: http://media.sermonindex.net/20/SID20193.mp3

The point is that despite all our shortcomings, and failures, and our multitude of sins, we are still considered by God to be holy, because Jesus is holy, and we are one with Him. Jesus' blood was able to provide a holiness that the blood of lambs was never able to bring. The Jews were expected to bring a pure lamb, so that it could take the punishment for their impurity. They took on the lamb's spotlessness, and the lamb took on their sin, and then died for it. Only now, Jesus has offered Himself as that sacrifice once and for all, on your behalf. That's why we don't need to keep bringing sacrifices to the temple, or killing lambs, because one great sacrifice has been made for everybody.

**"And by that will we have been sanctified through the offering of the body of Jesus Christ once for all. And every priest stands daily at his service, offering repeatedly the same sacrifices, which can never take away sins. But when Christ had offered for all time a single sacrifice for sins, he sat down at the right hand of God." (Hebrews 10:10-12)**

He Himself was the sacrifice - the pure, spotless lamb that had no blemish or defect - that was required of us. That is why when John the Baptist saw Him, he cried,

**"Behold, the Lamb of God, who takes away the sin of the world!" (John 1:29b)**

Jesus would be the lamb that was required for all people – the sacrifice once and for all. His holiness was accredited to us, the way the purity of a lamb used to be accredited to the person that brought it. There is no possible way for you to be any holier than you are in Christ. He is as holy as He possibly could be, and His holiness is accredited to you, through that divine mystery of grace we call propitiation. There is nothing you can do to make yourself more holy. You can't possibly be any more righteous than you are in Christ. Don't bother abstaining from pork, or trying to keep other Old Testament laws. Christ has done as much as could possibly be done, on your behalf. Don't add anything to that equation. Just believe in the purity of Christ.

"Who is a God like you, pardoning iniquity and passing over transgression for the remnant of His inheritance? He does not retain His anger forever, because He delights in steadfast love. He will again have compassion on us; He will tread our iniquities underfoot, You will cast all our sins into the depths of the sea. You will show faithfulness to Jacob and steadfast love to Abraham, as you have sworn to our fathers from the days of old." (Micah 7:18-20)

You *are* considered pure. You *are* considered holy, because Jesus is holy, and you are in Him, and He is in you.

### 3. Examining the part we play in the process of becoming holy

Not only has Christ made you holy once and for all, but He is making you holy. Although, legally, you are considered by God to be perfect because you are in Christ, at the same time, Christ is making you more like Himself as He dwells in you. In theological terms that's called Definitive Sanctification and Progressive Sanctification. Jesus has *made* you holy (Definitive), so that you can *become* holy (Progressive).

**"He himself bore our sins in his body on the tree, that we might die to sin and live to righteousness. By his wounds you have been healed." (1 Peter 2:24)**

As you live your Christian life, you are in the process of being made more like Jesus. That process is called sanctification. And it isn't achieved by trying harder, praying longer or going to church more. It comes through a deeper and better understanding of the fact that Jesus has already made you holy. And as you come to understand more of what Jesus has made you (legally) you begin to live out (on a day-to-day basis) those realities.

**"Since we have these promises, beloved, let us cleanse ourselves from every defilement of body and spirit, bringing holiness to completion in the fear of God." (2 Corinthians 7:1)**

Holiness is believing that Jesus has saved you from the power of sin, and living out that reality. That's the purest definition I can think to give you. Tchividjian, writing on a similar subject, says this,

"Our hard work, therefore, means coming to a greater understanding of *His* work. And so it is that we move further into the gospel, into a deeper, bigger, brighter understanding of all that God has already achieved for us in Christ. By continuing to place your trust in Christ's finished work, and by learning to do this more and more, all that He's secured for sinners – all that is your possession already in fact – now becomes yours increasingly in experience."[21]

So what does that look like on a practical, day to day level? How do we live out the realities of a risen Lord? Well, again, I don't have any formula or convenient checklist. But let's try to take this from being a concept, and put it into words that are more practical to everyday life. Kevin DeYoung has made this list of five things that holiness looks like.[22]

1. Holiness looks like the renewal of God's image.

- Holiness, basically, means being like God. If you want to know what holiness looks like, look at God.

2. Holiness looks like a life marked by virtue instead of vice

- Quite simply, we put off sin and put on righteousness. The Bible doesn't have any commands on how long to pray, but it has lots of lists on how to use your body in a pure, godly way. Holiness means putting to death the deeds of the flesh and putting on Christ.

3. Holiness looks like a clean conscience

- The little voice inside your head is not infallible, but the law *has* been written on your heart. So even though your Christian friends want you to watch a mostly-clean movie, or can thoroughly prove that the Bible

---

21   Tchividjian, Tullian. *Jesus + Nothing = Everything*. Wheaton, IL:Crossway, 2011. Print. p. 96.

22   DeYoung, Kevin. *The Hole in Our Holiness*. Wheaton, IL: Crossway, 2012. Print.p. 38-47 The five points are all his. The sub-points are my own paraphrase of his work.

never says anything about avoiding alcohol, if your conscience tells you not to do it, don't do it. Train yourself to listen to your conscience on the small, technical issues, and you won't find yourself trampling it on the bigger issues.

- It is possible to have a clear conscience and still sin (just go talk to a psychopath), so having a clean conscience is not a reason to go ahead with something. But having an unclean conscience is a reason not to go ahead with something.

4. Holiness looks like obedience to God's commands

- It sounds nice to say God is interested in relationships and not religion, but it isn't entirely Biblical. Keeping commands isn't legalism, its Christianity. You are not redeemed *by* obeying the law, but you are redeemed *to* obey it. If you still have doubts see 1 John 2:3-4

5. Holiness looks like Christ-likeness

- We see in Jesus the best, most practical, most human example of what it means to be holy. He is the ultimate example of how to live.

Jesus has rescued you from sin, and you are to live out that reality. Charles Spurgeon once wrote, "If Christ has died for me, ungodly as I am, without strength as I am, then I cannot live in sin any longer, but must arouse myself to love and serve Him who hath redeemed me, I cannot trifle with the evil which slew my best Friend. I must be holy for His sake. How can I live in sin when He has died to save me from it?"[23] Choose to listen to music that demonstrates what Jesus has saved you from, and what He is making you into. Choose what movies you watch according to the same standard. Before you speak, think about whether what you are saying is something that is using the breath God gave you in a beneficial way. I don't have any set guidelines for holy living. Just live a life that demonstrates the fact that you have been saved from sin. Don't entertain any of the things that put Jesus on the cross.

**Now the works of the flesh are evident: sexual immorality, impurity, sensuality, idolatry, sorcery, enmity, strife, jealousy, fits of anger, rivalries, dissensions, divisions, envy, drunkenness, orgies, and things like these. I warn you, as I warned you before, that those who do such things will not inherit the kingdom of God. But**

---

23  Spurgeon, Charles. *All of Grace.* Public Domain.

**the fruit of the Spirit is love, joy, peace, patience, kindness, goodness, faithfulness, gentleness, self-control; against such things there is no law. And those who belong to Christ Jesus have crucified the flesh with its passions and desires. If we live by the Spirit, let us also walk by the Spirit. (Galatians 5:19-25)**

When you try to be holy by obeying a set of rules, we call that legalism. And the reason legalism is so wrong is because by placing value on rules, you are saying that Jesus + Works = Holiness. But the only thing worse than legalism is antinomianism. That's the belief that no law is relevant or important – you can live however you want. And the reason that's so horrid, is because its like spitting in the face of Christ and choosing to live in the life He has saved you from.

It may have been wiser for me to have been like DeYoung and written a whole book on holiness, rather than a chapter. The subjects written about here feel hurried and incomplete, but sometimes the noblest truths come through the simplest means. So I pray that through this quick overview of a vast subject, you will have gleaned something you can apply to your life.

Let's just summarize quickly. God is holy – He is undefiled, and has nothing to do with sin. He has saved you from sin, and called you to be holy like He is. He doesn't want you running back to what He just saved you from. Sometimes you and I fall back into the sin He just rescued us from, but He is worthy and willing to redeem you, because it wasn't your holiness that gave you a relationship with Him anyways. Jesus is holy, and His holiness has been given to you, when you are unified with Him. You can't do anything to make yourself more holy than you are in Christ. But as you grow in an understanding of the purity Jesus has given you, you come to live out that reality. On a practical, day to day basis, you grow to look more like the holy Saviour that you are one with.

*Dear Father,*
*I pray that you would teach me about holiness*
*Help me to grow in my understanding of the holiness of Jesus*
*Teach me how to live a pure, undefiled life*

*Make me more holy*
*Make me more like you*
*Teach me how to live out the reality of a risen Lord*
*Reveal to me what unholy things in my life need to be dealt with*
*Search me, O God, and know my heart!*
*Try me, and show me if there be any wicked way in me.*
*In Jesus name,*
*Amen*

## Chapter 7: The Torn Veil

Mankind was made by God, and for God. And more than that, we were made to enjoy God. The Westminster catechism states that, "Man's chief end is to glorify God, and to enjoy him for ever." The simple truth is that Jesus did not die on the cross to save us from hell, give us rules and then put us into churches to serve Him by doing mundane tasks. He saved us, gave us new hearts that are *able* to love and adore Him, that *desire* to have an intimacy with Him, and that *choose* to enjoy living in His Presence forever. We glorify Him as we enjoy Him.

We were made to live, and to enjoy living, in the Presence of God. The Presence of God is something we've fled from right from the beginning. God created Adam in the garden for His own glory, and pleasure, and Adam spent His days walking with God, enjoying communion, and glorifying God by enjoying God's Presence. But Adam fled from the garden where God Himself walked in the cool of the day, and we've been fleeing ever since. Not that we can really flee from God, because He fills the whole Earth.

**"Am I a God at hand, declares the LORD, and not a God far away? Can a man hide himself in secret places so that I cannot see him? declares the LORD. Do I not fill heaven and earth? declares the LORD." (Jeremiah 23:23-24)**

But, as we discussed in chapter 5, there is a difference between knowing God and *knowing* God. You can know Him as your saviour, and then you can *know* Him as you draw near to His heart. Adam *knew* God – he stood in God's manifest presence, but it was the manifest Presence that he fled, and spent his life merely in God's omnipresence. And God has been trying to restore that relationship with us ever since.

If you have no desire for a nearness to God, I have no message for you. If you believe, for some reason, that once a person knows God they know Him as intimately as they ever will, there is nothing here for you. But if you have a hunger for deeper things – if you have a desire to walk closely with God, and to enjoy Him forever, then have faith. You were made to enjoy God, and He rewards those who seek the pleasure of walking closely with Him.

**"And without faith it is impossible to please him, for whoever would draw near to God must believe that he exists and that he rewards those who seek him." (Hebrews 11:6)**

Adam had a relationship with God, but when he disobeyed, he was thrust from the Lord's Presence. And God's work of redemption has been to undo everything that Adam did. Not just to take away the death that Adam deserved, but also to restore the communion that God once had with man.

Prior to the cross, God's Presence dwelt in what was called the Holy of Holies, or the Most Holy Place. The Holy of Holies was a room that was a perfect cube[24] and overlaid with pure gold.[25] It was guarded by a thick purple and blue curtain that had pictures of cherubim sewed into it.[26] The ark of the covenant was in that room, and God sat on a throne between the two cherubim on its lid.[27] Only the High Priest could enter into the Holy of Holies,[28] and that was only once a year. But once he went beyond the curtain, he was standing again in the Presence of God, as Adam had once done.

That was the true glory of the tabernacle. God was there. Not that the rest of Israel was outside of God's Presence, but the Holy of Holies was distinguished as the place where God sat upon His throne. Only the High Priest could enter that throne room, until Jesus came and entered once and for everyone.

---

24   Just like the New Jerusalem - Revelation 21:16

25   Eden, where God's Presence dwelt, was also filled with gold - Genesis 2:12, as heaven will be - Revelation 21:18

26   Exodus 26:1-2. Eden's entrance was also guarded by a cherubim – Genesis 3:24.

27   Exodus 25:22, 2 Samuel 6:2, Isaiah 37:16

28   When God was on Mount Sinai, only one man (Moses) could come up the mountain. Anyone else would be killed. Exodus 19:10-13, Exodus 19:20

**"But when Christ appeared as a high priest of the good things that have come, then through the greater and more perfect tent (not made with hands, that is, not of this creation) he entered once for all into the holy places, not by means of the blood of goats and calves but by means of his own blood, thus securing an eternal redemption." (Hebrews 9:11-12)**

A high priest is no longer required to stand and offer sacrifices there, because Jesus has entered with a more perfect sacrifice (Himself) on behalf of everyone. When Jesus died, the curtain that guards the Holy of Holies was torn, top to bottom,[29] because God's Presence was no longer confined to that room, but was available to all men.

**"Therefore, brothers, since we have confidence to enter the holy places by the blood of Jesus, by the new and living way that he opened for us through the curtain, that is, through his flesh, and since we have a great priest over the house of God, let us draw near with a true heart in full assurance of faith, with our hearts sprinkled clean from an evil conscience and our bodies washed with pure water." (Hebrews 10:19-22)**

Because of Christ, we can confidently come into the Holy of Holies. We can shamelessly stand in the Presence of God. We are invited, in Christ, to come near before God.

**"Draw near to God, and He will draw near to you. Cleanse your hands, you sinners, and purify your hearts, you double-minded." (James 4:8)**

**"But I, through the abundance of your steadfast love, will enter your house. I will bow down toward your holy temple in the fear of you." (Psalm 5:7)**

You were born a son of Adam, hiding from the Presence because of your sin, but you have become a Son of God, through Jesus, who

---

[29] Matthew 27:51, Mark 15:37-38, Luke 23:45-46

...d with boldness right back into the Presence. We now have not confidence to enter into the Holy of Holies, but an invitation.

...W. Tozer (who is far more qualified to write on this subject than I am) was literally on his knees when he wrote his classic book *The Pursuit of God*. He writes,

"The interior journey of the soul from the wilds of sin into the enjoyed Presence of God is beautifully illustrated in the Old Testament tabernacle. The returning sinner first entered the outer court where he offered a blood sacrifice on the brazen altar and washed himself in the laver that stood near it. Then through a veil he passed into the holy place where no natural light could come, but the golden candlestick which spoke of Jesus the Light of the World threw its soft glow over all. There also was the shewbread to tell of Jesus, the Bread of Life, and the altar of incense, a figure of unceasing prayer.

Though the worshipper had enjoyed so much, still he had not yet entered the Presence of God. Another veil separated from the Holy of Holies where above the mercy seat dwelt the very God Himself in awful and glorious manifestation. While the tabernacle stood, only the high priest could enter there, and that but once a year, with blood which he offered for his sins and the sins of the people. It was this last veil which was rent when our Lord gave up the ghost on Calvary, and the sacred writer explains that this rending of the veil opened the way for every worshipper in the world to come by the new and living way straight into the divine Presence.

Everything in the New Testament accords with this Old Testament picture. Ransomed men need no longer pause in fear to enter the Holy of Holies. God wills that we should push on into His Presence and live our whole life there. This is to be known to us in conscious experience. It is more than a doctrine to be held, it is a life to be enjoyed every moment of every day."[30]

Not just on a doctrinal level, but in physical, practical experience, man's chief end is to glorify God and enjoy Him forever. I'm not speaking of mysticism, or emotion, or fantasy experiences. I do speak from experience, but the Word of God is a greater authority than

---

[30] Tozer, A.W. *The Pursuit of God*. Harrisburg, PA: Christian Publications, Inc., Copyright MCMXLVIII. PDF Document. p. 11.

experience, so the only experience that can stand is experience that can be affirmed in Scripture. A way has been made into the Holy of Holies, but quite often Christians are content to have Christ offered as a sacrifice on the altar, to be washed in the bronze basin (or laver), and then to spend their life in the courtyard of the tabernacle. God invites you to draw near, but you feel far more comfortable and safe to dwell at a distance, and observe God's manifest Presence without ever partaking. But to those who would give up their safety, and the comfort of their courtyard experience as a Christian, comes this cry:

**Sow for yourselves righteousness; reap steadfast love; *break up your fallow ground,* for it is the time to seek the LORD, that he may come and rain righteousness upon you. (Hosea 10:12, emphasis added)**

A fallow field, is, in simple terms, one that has never been ploughed. It is quiet and safe, and is probably covered with a thin layer of grass, and perhaps a few bushes. That is a picture of one kind of Christian life, and perhaps it is a picture of your life. It is fallow – safe, and untouched by the fiery vibrancy provided by the work of the cold, hard plough. Don't misunderstand me, it is not a picture of a carnal Christian life, for there *is* life in a fallow field. There is life in a fallow Christian, there is a desire for God's Word, and a recognition of the importance of prayer, and the fallow Christian has perhaps even led others to Christ. It is not a lifeless field, but it is still a fallow field. But when the plough comes, and destroys whatever comfort and life the fallow Christian had, seeds of righteousness are laid and there is life a hundredfold. The fruit produced by a ploughed field is exponentially more abundant than the fruit produced in a fallow field. Righteousness is laid in the tilled ground, and steadfast love is reaped.

And so it is with us. Christ has made a way for us to step beyond the fallow life found in the courtyard, and has offered a life of abundance in the Presence of the Almighty. But the way Christ made into the Holy of Holies was the cross, and that remains the only way. The cross, much like the plough, is a cold, hard, killing machine that has no interest in comfort or luxury. Both are very real tools – neither is useful as a concept, but only in actual application. The cross searches through the life the way a plough digs into the ground, and uproots that which is unproductive, lazy and mostly asleep. The cross is not concerned with how you justify the various ways you have spent your time – it isn't worried about the little things that have been accomplished for God through your actions – but uproots everything, both good and bad, seeking to plant a greater and more abundant seed.

And this ploughing - this cold hard cross, is the path out of the courtyard and into the Holy of Holies. The comfort and safety of an ordinary life are done away with. Sleep is exchanged for prayer, time with friends is exchanged for time with the Word, and a life of self-suiting plans is exchanged for a life of ministry (and ministry, just for the record, does not necessarily mean being a pastor, missionary or soup kitchen worker. It means being Christ to everyone around you, in season and out of season). Like all processes, God plays a part, and man plays a part. The plough is God's – the ploughing and the breaking are a work of God. But man chooses the plough, asks God for the plough, and consents to let God continue ploughing on a daily basis.

When you get serious with God, He will get serious with you. When you seek to *know* Him, He is willing to be found. When you draw near to God, He will draw near to you.

In 1892, there was a man named John Hyde who graduated from seminary and went to India, to be a missionary. He wasn't planning on being a missionary when he went into seminary, but God's plough had no interest in his plans. He went to the Punjab people – one of five missionaries in the midst of almost one million non-Christians. When Hyde arrived in India, rather than diving into language studies, he began to study the Scriptures. 'First things first,' he said.[31] He had come to preach the Bible, and figured he needed to know it before he could preach it. John Hyde threw aside whatever hobbies, interests or luxuries he could have been enjoying in his free time, and decided to enjoy God. He drew near to God, and God drew near to him.

Hyde began a yearly convention in India for pastors, teachers and evangelists. In preparation for this event, Hyde and two other men spent thirty days and thirty nights praying for an outpouring of God's

---

31      Carre, Captain E.G. *Praying Hyde*. Alachu, FL: Bridge-Logos, 2011. Print. p. 6.

power. "Three human hearts that beat as one and that one the heart of Christ, yearning, pleading, praying, and agonizing over the Church of India and the myriads of lost souls."[32] Life in the courtyard was not enough for Hyde. Jesus had made a way into the Holy of Holies, and Hyde would be satisfied with nothing less. He wanted all of God.

There was great power at that convention, as God drew near to His people. And God drew near to His people, because three of His people had drawn near to Him. They had prayed, rather than slept, for thirty days. Praying, rather than sleeping, doesn't exactly sound like a fallow, comfortable field to me. But not only had they drawn near to God through hours of prayer, they had drawn near in the purity of Christ the lamb. The plough had destroyed their sleeping patterns, but it had also destroyed their sin lives. Hyde had once struggled with sin, even as a Christian. Years before, he had written this,

"I knew there was a sin in my life that had not been taken away. I realized what a dishonor it would be on the name of Christ to have to confess that I was preaching a Christ that had not delivered me from sin, though I was proclaiming to others that He was a perfect Saviour. I went back to my room and shut myself in, and told the Lord that it must be one of two things: either He must give me victory over all my sins, and especially the sin that so easily beset me, or I must return to America and seek there for some other work."[33]

The Lord had given Hyde deliverance, and clothed in holiness, he had marched right up to the throne of God and spent the rest of his life living at His feet. But he had come in holiness, and this is one of the great secrets we often miss in North America.

**"Strive for peace with everyone, and for the holiness without which no one will see the Lord" (Hebrews 12:14)**

---

[32]    Carre, Captain E.G. *Praying Hyde*. Alachu, FL: Bridge-Logos, 2011. Print. p. 8-9.

[33]    Carre, Captain E.G. *Praying Hyde*. Alachu, FL: Bridge-Logos, 2011. Print. p. 53.

rags, and I, in faith, claim His righteousness. Now, a twofold result follows: As to our Father in heaven, He sees Christ's righteousness – not my unrighteousness. A second result as to ourselves: Christ's righteousness not merely clothes us outwardly, but enters into our very being, by His Spirit, received in faith, as with the disciples (see John 20:22), and works out sanctification in us."[35]

So if you want to experience the fullness of the life God has given you, if you want to live in the Presence of God, if you want to live a holy life, you have to begin with the understanding that you can not. Only Jesus can do that. He is the High Priest who enters into the Holy of Holies, and the only confidence we have that we can draw near, is in the fact that we are one with Him.

**"Since then we have a great high priest who has passed through the heavens, Jesus, the Son of God, let us hold fast our confession. For we do not have a high priest who is unable to sympathize with our weaknesses, but one who in every respect has been tempted as we are, yet without sin. Let us then with confidence draw near to the throne of grace, that we may receive mercy and find grace to help in time of need." (Hebrews 4:14-16)**

The plough is waiting to rearrange your schedule. The cross is waiting, to crucify you again. Hyde challenged his fellow believers to spend at least half an hour in prayer each day, as close after noon as possible. What would it look like if you threw out whatever you normally do in that time, and prayed for God to awaken you? Prayed for God to awaken those around you? I don't know your life, and I don't know your time, but look through the things you do each day and ask yourself what life would look like if you threw something out and spent that time in prayer, instead. Prayer time doesn't materialize magically. If you're going to gain it, you're going to have to give up time doing something else.

John Hyde spent so many long hours in intercession, he eventually died. He prayed with such passion that his body couldn't take the strain.

---

35    Carre, Captain E.G. *Praying Hyde*. Alachu, FL: Bridge-Logos, 2011. Print. p. 21.

After years of sharing God's grief for a fallen world, Hyde had toiled so hard in prayer that his heart had physically shifted to the wrong side of his body. The doctors prescribed months of rest, but Hyde couldn't stop seeking God. He literally prayed himself to death. He was 46 when he died.

Are you dying to live? Ask God for the plough. Ask Him for the cross. Man was made to glorify God and enjoy Him forever. Don't spend another day outside of the fullness of God's manifest Presence. The veil has been torn, do not live another day outside of it.

*Father of Our Great High Priest,*

*We thank you that you have made a way through the curtain.*

*We thank you that you have made a way for us to come before your throne without fear.*

*I pray that you would teach me to come clothed with Jesus' righteousness alone.*

*Rearrange my life Lord,*

*Break up my daily routine, and shatter the comfort in my life.*

*I give up the life where I am for the sake of having a life in your Presence.*

*Break me with kindness and crucify me with love.*

*I want to dwell in the Holy of Holies.*

*In the name of the Great High Priest,*

*Jesus Christ,*

*Amen.*

## Chapter 8: Giving Back

Loving God and loving others are inseparable concepts, and both will flow from a heart that understands how generously God gives to His children. God is not only a God of infinite majesty, unending love, incomparable glory and indescribable splendour, but a God who continually shares all His majesty, love, glory and splendour with His children. You'll never really appreciate the magnificence of God until you understand how generously He pours out His magnificence on a people that do not deserve it. God is full of goodness, and His goodness flows into you like an unending stream. When you come to God, whether through studying Scripture, through prayer time, through worship in music, or through whatever else, He has an immeasurable wealth of goodness and steadfast love, that He is not only willing, but desiring to satisfy you with, to such a level that you will rejoice and be glad all your life for His goodness towards you.[36]

**"Blessed be the God and Father of our Lord Jesus Christ, who has blessed us in Christ with *every* spiritual blessing in the heavenly places." (Ephesians 1:3, emphasis added)**

**"In Him we have redemption through His blood, the forgiveness of our trespasses, according to the riches of His grace, which he lavished upon us in all wisdom and insight." (Ephesians 1:7-8)**

**"Having the eyes of our hearts enlightened, that you may know what is the hope to which He has called you, what are the riches of His glorious inheritance in the saints, and what is the immeasurable greatness of His power toward us who believe, according to the work of His great might." (Ephesians 1:18-19)**

God's riches are lavished upon you. He is never short on goodness He is willing to share, but is generous far beyond what we deserve. One of the most important truths for you to grasp is that God's mercy will never run out for the repentant. He is not an impatient God. His goodness just keeps flowing out to those who keep coming to Him. He is willing to restore in you an abundant joy, even when you plunge

---

[36] Psalm 90:14

yourself back into all the joy-stealing misery that He saved you from.[37] We serve a good God, who is never reserved in sharing any of His goodness, but pours out grace, mercy and love upon us, day after day, even though you never earned a drop of it.

We have been drawn out of slavery into His family. You are alive in Christ. This mean you are His child, and a co-heir with Christ. We do not need to work to earn His wealth, but are already rich in Him.[38] It is in His nature to give of His nature. The love, mercy, grace and patience of the Father is given freely to His children. This is why one of the most important things in your life is to know and understand the character of God.

**"The fear of the Lord is the beginning of wisdom, and the knowledge of the Holy One is insight." (Proverbs 9:10)**

When you understand who God is, you will understand precisely what He gives to the Christian, because He gives according to who He is. His characteristics and His gifts go hand in hand. When you understand just how glorious He is, you will understand just how immeasurable the riches He gives to you are. When I was a toddler and I drew a picture for my mom, she would hang it on the fridge, and I would be thrilled that my mom was willing to display my art. I gave it, she displayed it, and I was instantly in 4 year old heaven. God delights in seeing people carrying out all the characteristics of Himself that He lavished on them.

**"But let him who boasts boast in this, that he understands and knows me, that I am the LORD who practices steadfast love, justice, and righteousness in the earth. For in these things I delight, declares the LORD." (Jeremiah 9:24)**

God's steadfast love is lavished upon His children as if we were large empty cups and He were a pitcher that just poured and poured into us.

---

[37] Psalm 51:12

[38] That is to say, we are wealthy in our knowledge of God, and our enjoyment of Him. This does not mean wealthy as in prosperous or monetarily successful. I do not mean to imply that God is going to fill your bank account.

He never stops pouring His love out upon you. Every time you find somewhere to pray alone, He cares about you as if you were the only one in the world talking to Him. He sees, recognizes and cares for *every* need of His children – there is no physical pain or financial difficulty or emotional trouble that is overlooked by Him. He may not swoop in and meet your every need in precisely the way you expect, but He does care for you, and certainly does not overlook a single hardship.

But being 'alive in Christ' does not simply mean receiving all that God gives to you. Sanctification – the process of becoming more like Christ – is about giving back to God, and to other people, everything that God has given you. So you take that cup - your life - that God keeps pouring into, and you pour it back out to Him, and into the lives of everyone you come into contact with. Loving God and loving others fulfils all of the Old Testament law.[39] The greatest joy in life is not in receiving God's love and goodness, but letting His love and goodness pour out of you, and seeing that He replenishes it a hundredfold, so that you may continue pouring it out.

One of the biggest issues for worship leaders is ensuring that worship time is God-centred and not self-centred. Its easy for people to get lost in the emotion and the excitement of a worship evening, and bask in the warm fuzzy feelings they are receiving (you can argue somewhere else about whether or not warm fuzzy feelings are from God – it is irrelevant to this teaching). Worship time can become primarily a time of selfishness when it becomes simply about your own enjoyment. How do we balance enjoyment of God with selflessness? God does desire for you to be both satisfied by His love and to enjoy His Presence, and this is not selfishness when all the goodness you receive overflows from you into others. It is not selfishness to (figuratively speaking) run to God's banqueting table and stuff your mouth and pockets with food, if you are running to others to share it with them, or using the energy you got from that meal to serve others.

Worship is enjoying and soaking up all of God's goodness and giving Him all the glory for it, and then taking all that you have soaked up to a world in need. So true Godliness is not just knowing that your every

---

[39] Luke 10:26-28, Mark 12:29-33, Romans, 13:8-10

breath is a gift from God – it is using every breath you have to glorify Him and tell others about Him. Godliness is not just knowing that God loves you. Godliness is loving the Lord your God with all your heart, soul, strength and mind, and loving your neighbour as yourself. Godliness is taking everything that God has given you, and pouring it back out to Him, and to others.

David does this once in the Old Testament. His men risked their lives to bring him a cup of beautiful, fresh water from Bethlehem. And what did He do with it? He poured it out to God.

**"And David said longingly, "Oh that someone would give me water to drink from the well of Bethlehem that is by the gate!" Then the three mighty men broke through the camp of the Philistines and drew water out of the well of Bethlehem that was by the gate and took it and brought it to David. But David would not drink it. He poured it out to the LORD." (1 Chronicles 11:17-18).**

You may not have water from Bethlehem – but you have Jesus, the living water in your soul. That precious, beautiful water is not in a cup handed to you by soldiers, but in your heart, and you would do well to not let all the richness and goodness of that living water to grow stagnant inside of you. Let Christ pour out of you for the world to see. There is another classic example of this in the New Testament, when Mary poured out perfume of great value at Jesus' feet.

**"Mary therefore took a pound of expensive ointment made from pure nard, and anointed the feet of Jesus and wiped his feet with her hair. The house was filled with the fragrance of the perfume." (John 12:3)**

Mary took something precious and valuable – something God had blessed her with – and she poured it out to Him. And in this, she experienced the greater blessing of the Saviour. God had blessed her with something physically valuable, but it was not having received that blessing from God that marked her as a Godly woman, but pouring it back out to Him marked her as someone who understood what it meant to love the Saviour.

All that God has given you should be given back to the glory of God, and used for the blessing of others. This is the beginning of coming alive in Christ. And in doing this, you will fulfil the heart of the law, which is summarized in the two great commandments,

**"You shall Love the Lord your God with all your heart, soul, strength and mind." (Deuteronomy 6:5, Matthew 22:37, Mark 12:30, Luke 10:27)**

and

**"Love your neighbour as yourself." (Leviticus 19:8, Matthew 22:39, Mark 12:31, Luke 10:27)**

The minor prophets are the books of the Bible that are often remembered for talking so frequently about the wrath of God. Why is God so angry with Israel during those times? Primarily, for two reasons – improper worship, and improperly treating their fellow countrymen. They didn't love Him, and they didn't love others. He had blessed them immeasurably, and their hearts were so hard, they did not honour Him, or treat others as He had treated them, and for this He was angry.

God has forgiven you time and time again. Forgive others. God has loved you immeasurably. Love others. God has cared about your pain, and your needs. Care about others. Take a moment to stop and think about all the things God has ever done in your life. Thank Him and then use the life He has given you to do the same unto others, to the best of your ability. Whatever God has given you, should be poured back out. Pick your Bible up again and look up Luke 19:12-27 (seriously!).

Luke. Read.

Whether God has given a lot, or a little, whatever you have been given should not be saved and cherished, but invested. The Christian life ought to be marked by a true and genuine love that flows out of a heart dedicated to serving God. It should be the sincerity of our worship and the genuine humility of our acts of servanthood that attracts others to us.

D.A. Carson once wrote, "We increasingly inhabit a time and place in Western history when humility is perceived to be a sign of weakness; when meekness is taken for a vice, not a virtue; when puff is more important than substance; when leadership, even in the church, frequently has more to do with politics, pizazz and showmanship, or with structure and hierarchy, than with spiritual maturity and conformity to Jesus Christ; when the budget is thought to be a more important indicator of ecclesiastical success than prayerfulness, and when loose talk of spiritual experience wins an instant following, even when that talk is mingled with a scarcely concealed haughtiness that has learned neither humility nor tears."[40]

Let God's character, and not human priorities shape who you are. You were made in God's image, and that is the only image you were intended to reflect. Do not let the standards and expectations of the world (or even the church) define your actions. Let your actions be defined by how God has acted towards you. He has treated you according to the character you were designed to reflect.

God is a rich God! He owns the cattle on a thousand hills,[41] He offers wine, milk and honey without price,[42] and He will feed you freely with knowledge and understanding.[43] There is no end to God's riches. What He is, He gives, and He gives without price. So three things are terribly important for you. 1) To know and understand the character of God. 2) To recognize and believe that God is a giving God, and all of His goodness is given to you. 3) You ought to take all that God has given you and pour it back out to Him and into others.

God has been so loving and so kind to us. Lay down yourself, take up Christ and then live Christ to everyone around you. Love the Lord your

---

[40] Carson, D.A. *A Model of Christian Maturity*. Grand Rapids, MI: Baker Book House Company, 2007. Print. p. 13.

[41] Psalm 50:10

[42] Isaiah 55:1

[43] Jeremiah 3:15

God with all your heart, soul, strength and mind. Love your neighbour as yourself.

*Dear Father,*
*You have been so good to me,*
*I thank you for your mercy, which is new every morning,*
*and for your grace, which I could never earn.*
*I pray that you would teach me how to be to others as you are to me.*
*May your love define my life.*
*May I be Christ-like to those around me.*
*Teach me to love you.*
*Teach me to love others.*
*In Jesus name,*
*Amen.*

## Chapter 9: Alive in Christ

Neither pomp nor pizazz is important in Christian ministry – the heart is important. I want to go back to the quote reportedly from St. Francis of Assisi that was used at the very beginning of this book. "Preach the Gospel always, and if necessary, use words." He was one of history's biggest advocates for social justice – feeding the hungry, clothing the poor and so on. And while that is mandated by Scripture and crucial to our ministries, I believe that living the gospel goes far beyond just that. How you conduct yourself before others will be your greatest testimony of the gospel. In the early 1800s, revivalist Charles Finney wrote this,

"People act on others by language, looks, tears and daily conduct. Take, for example, an unrepentant man, one who has a spiritual wife – her looks, tenderness, her solemn, compassionate dignity softened and molded into the image of Christ are to him a continuous sermon. He turns his mind away because it is such a reproach to him, yet a sermon rings in his ears all day long. We all read people. Sinners often read the state of a Christian's mind in his eyes. If his eyes are full of lightness or anxiousness or scheming, sinners see it. If his eyes are full of the Spirit of God, sinners read it and are often convicted just by seeing the facial expressions of Christians."[44]

How do you *live* the Christian life? How do you have eyes that people read and see God behind? How do you move beyond just surviving as a Christian that avoids major sin? How do you grow into a life that proclaims the gospel with power, that has victory over every entangling sin? How do you become a soldier and not merely a spectator? How do you love and serve others as Christ did? How do you *live* (not merely exist) this Christian life of pouring back to God and to others? The answer to those questions is the main thrust and message of this book.

**"Consider yourselves dead to sin and alive to God in Christ Jesus." (Romans 6:11)**

---

[44] Finney, Charles G., ed. Kevin Walter Johnson. *Lectures on Revival.* Minneapolis, MN. Bethany House Publishers. 1988. Print.

Lay down your sin. Lay down your self. Give everything you are, over to God. Surrender. Give up. Die. Let go of sin. Let go of everything you hold onto. And then come alive. Pursue Him. Enter into His Presence. Be holy as He is holy. And let Him live in you and through you. Let His love, and His character pour through you. Learn to love Him with all your heart, soul, strength and mind. Let His love consume you until you learn to love others as yourself. Let the John the Baptist's words be your prayer as you live the Christian life:

**"He must increase, but I must decrease" (John 3:30).**

Charles Spurgeon once wrote, "Inconsistent professing Christians injure the gospel more than the sneering critic or or the heretic."[45] Let your conduct on this earth be representative of the Risen Saviour in your heart. Live out all that Christ has called you to.

Talking about being alive in Christ is easy enough. Preaching the gospel with your life and not merely your words is a nice concept, but what does that look like on a practical, day to day basis? In the daily muck of life, what does it look like to pour all that God has given out into others? The answer to both those questions is beautifully articulated all throughout Scripture, but I think Paul cuts it out plain and simple in Romans 12. I want to break down that chapter and make it as practical as I can. But I also want to make it clear that Scripture speaks plainly enough for itself. Please do not skim over the verses in this chapter (or in the rest of the book!). Please read them carefully, and consider their meaning for your life. As I wrote in the preface (which you probably skipped!), Scripture is far, far more important than my words. I'll try to add some practical advice beneath each verse, but the brunt of the message is in the verses. Read them carefully.

**"I appeal to you therefore brothers, by the mercies of God, to present your bodies as a living sacrifice, holy and acceptable to God, which is your spiritual worship." (Romans 12:1)**

---

45 Spurgeon, C.H., ed. Alistair Begg. *Morning and Evening with Spurgeon.* New Kensington, PA. Whitaker House. 2001. Print. May 17, morning.

Can it be more clear than that? Take all that defines your life, and lay it on God's altar. He will do more with you surrendered and tied up on an altar than you ever will with all the effort of an untied man running circles around the altar trying to accomplish things himself.

**"Do not be conformed to this world, but be transformed by the renewal of your mind, that by testing you may discern what is the will of God, what is good and acceptable and perfect." (Romans 12:2)**

Being conformed to the pattern of the world means looking and acting like everyone else. You can know that you are conformed to the world if somebody could watch the group of friends you hang out with and not be able to pick out which one of you is a Christian. Being conformed to the world means loving, and finding joy and fulfilment in the same things that everybody else does. Charles Spurgeon once wrote this,

"If you desire to be on fire for God, realize that your love will be dampened by the cold rain of a godless society. You cannot become a great Christian, you can never be a mature believer in Christ Jesus while you give in to godless maxims and modes of life. It is incongruous for an heir of heaven to be a great friend with the heirs of hell. It is a bad look when the servant is too intimate with the king's enemies. Even small inconsistencies are dangerous. Just as small thorns make great blisters and little moths destroy fine clothes, so little frivolities and little indiscretions will rob your testimony of a thousand joys."[46]

Being transformed means changing day by day more into God's image. It is a continuing process of decreasing as He increases in your life, so that every day you are a little less like the 'you' that you were yesterday, and a little more like Jesus.

---

[46] Spurgeon, C.H., ed. Alistair Begg. *Morning and Evening with Spurgeon.* New Kensington, PA. Whitaker House. 2001. Print. October 14, evening.

When we become conformed to the patterns of this world, we lose sight of who God is. God's holiness is in such fierce opposition with the sin of this world that becoming accustomed and acquainted with the sinfulness of the world means making yourself an enemy of God.[47] As you fall into habits of sin, and begin to look and act like everyone else, you lose sight of who God is, and you lose your ability to discern His will. You will become dulled to his standards of right and wrong, and unable to hear His voice directing your life. When you were saved, you were raised to new life, but when you begin to entertain sin again, you return to acting like the dead man you once were, and dead men can not hear! What is good, acceptable and perfect, is not revealed to those who are cold towards His demands for a sacrificed life, but is discerned by those who are being transformed into His likeness.

Notice that this verse is in two parts. The first tells you who you ought to be – not conformed, but being transformed and renewed. The second part talks about being able to discern the will of God. Quite often we want to be able to discern the will of God for the specifics in our lives without being willing to accept the commandment that comes first, which is to offer your body as a living sacrifice. Don't go flipping through the Bible asking God where He wants you to go to University or where He wants you to work, until you have dwelt on and understood His commandment to give your body as a living sacrifice. In flipping through your Bible looking for Him to tell you the specifics, you will have passed verse after verse about being dead to sin and surrendered to Christ. According to Romans 12:2, those are the prerequisites to being able to discern the will of God.

Offer yourself as living sacrifice, holy and acceptable to God. This is God's will for your life. Don't pass over these verses and skip to discerning God's will for the specifics of your life. Laying everything that you are on God's altar must come first, and from this offering will flow the ability to discern God's good, acceptable and perfect will. Essentially, you must pour yourself out to God before you can understand what it means to live in Christ, or pour love into other people. It is only after laying this foundation that Paul moves on to the specifics of 'living in Christ.'

---

[47]    James 4:4

**"For by the grace given to me I say to everyone among you not to think of himself more highly than he ought to think," (Romans 12:3a)**

Again, the foundational principle of successful ministry is decreasing so that Christ can increase. If you want to be a witness in this world, you must learn to walk humbly, not thinking of yourself more highly than you ought. The first sign of a hardened heart is an unwillingness to learn. If you feel that you know Scripture well enough that your pastor or youth leader doesn't have anything to teach you anymore, you are thinking of yourself more highly than you ought. A true man of God will appreciate any time the Word of God is opened, and be blessed to dwell on the richness of even the simplest of truths.

**"But to think with sober judgement, each according to the measure of faith that God has given you" (Romans 12:3b).**

When you come to a place where you consider yourself able and ready to stand up to temptation, you are prone to fall. Many Christian young people are willing to watch and listen to incredibly smutty things, feeling that they are strong enough that they can handle some degree of sin. Have the humility to admit that even the taint of sin can often leave thoughts in your mind that may grow later. It is always safer to walk carefully in the way of holiness than to attempt to stand strong on the edge of the precipice of sin. Never underestimate how easily sin entangles. Living in Christ – discerning the will of God – means discerning with proper judgement the sin you are to avoid.

**"For as in one body we have many members, and the members do not all have the same function, so we, though many are one body in Christ, and individually members one of another" (Romans 12:4-5)**

Part of coming alive in Christ is learning to enjoy the fellowship of others who God is also working in. God has given us the church for a reason – we all need each other. An unbeliever will never inspire you or encourage you in your pursuit of godliness the way other believers will. This is why in 2 Corinthians 6 Paul warns us not be yoked with unbelievers in any serious friendship, partnership or relationship (He isn't suggesting we are never to speak to unbelievers – just that you should not be restricted by your affections). Church gives us the opportunity to pray, worship and study with others who are also in a pursuit of God. Learn from the old, wise and experienced people you know, and encourage and spur on those who are running as you are. The church ought to be a group of believers, who are collectively in a constant pursuit of God, daily encouraging one another to keep their eyes on the prize. Like a sports team trains together and spurs each other on to athletic success, so too the church must encourage and spur each other on as we all run this spiritual race together.


**"Having gifts that differ according to the grace given to us, let us use them: if prophecy, in proportion to our faith; if service, in our serving; the one who teaches, in his teaching; the one who exhorts, in his exhortation; the one who contributes, in generosity; the one who leads, with zeal; the one who does acts of mercy, with cheerfulness." (Romans 12:6-8)**


Whatever gifts God has given you, use them for Him, and use them to bless others. Some of you reading this are people persons, and some of you are not. Some of you are comfortable on stage speaking to a crowd, some of you would rather speak one on one. Whatever ways God has gifted you, use those gifts to the full extent for Him. And don't think that the way you are talented is the way the whole church should be. Everyone has their own set of gifts to use for God. The preacher gifted in preaching couldn't preach if the church hydro bill hadn't been paid by someone gifted in generosity. Whether you are a giver, a preacher, or anything else, contribute your gift to the glory of God. And don't get hung up on only having one gift, or only contributing in one way. Strive to excel at all the things that are listed here – just know that you will just be naturally better at some than at others. What God has given you, give back to Him.


**"Let love be genuine." (Romans 12:9a)**


Love. It would take more than one book to unpack this little sentence. I'll just outline some thoughts that will help you as you further study the topic on your own. God is love. And, as was said in the last chapter, whatever God *is*, is what God *gives*. So God is loving, because God is love. He gives His love to you, and you are to give that love to others. That same, unconditional love that never fails and comes despite who you are and what you've done, is to be shown to other people. The culture we live in may have twisted and misused the word love, but Biblically, love is more than just an emotional response, it is an action. It would do you well to read and study the very commonly used verses in 1 Corinthians 13. In that passage, you will find two things. 1. A beautiful picture of precisely how God has acted towards you, and 2. a beautiful picture of how you are to act towards others.

**"Abhor what is evil, hold fast to what is good." (Romans 12:9b)**

If there's one verse in the Bible that needs to be painted on every wall of my room, its this. Because man, do we forget this simple command easily. What does it mean to be alive in Christ? In many ways, it is summed up in this verse. How do you preach the gospel with your life? By obeying this simple commandment. Don't just recognize what sin is – abhor it. Hate what is wrong! It doesn't mean hiding in a cave where you can never encounter wrong things – it means having a heart-change that makes you into someone who despises sin and loves God instead.

And hold fast to what is good. That means fighting for the things in your life worth fighting for! Like time in the morning reading your Bible. Your time spent in prayer. Sunday morning church time, which is easily swallowed by work and other things. Fight for it! Hold fast to what is good. Hold fast to that which transforms you by the renewing of your mind.

**Love one another with brotherly affection. Outdo one another in showing honour." (Romans 12:10)**

Brotherly love is not selfish. You don't love others because you get anything out of it. Care for other believers – recognize each others' needs, share each others burdens and pray for one another. Just as with siblings, you have an inseparable bond that will never end. My biological brother is going to be my brother forever, and so it is very important that there are no lasting quarrels between us – I must honour him. In the same way, your spiritual siblings will be your siblings forever – ensure there are no quarrels between you. And just for the record – this commandment is still relevant to you when you are in a relationship. Until the day you are married, you are to love your boyfriend or girlfriend as a sibling in Christ, and, as a little side note, I would suggest you go no farther physically than you would with your sibling. Simply love each other with brotherly affection, not with lustful, romantic affection.

**"Do not be slothful in zeal, be fervent in Spirit." (Romans 12:11)**

Do not be lazy, but be ready, willing, and quick to serve others, for God has never been slothful in taking notice of *your* needs (despite what you may think). What He has done for you, do to others. Be a servant of all, as Christ was. Lift ministering to others above your own recognition, comfort or fun. You will only be doing to others what God did to others when He was on earth. Excessive laziness and tiredness is one of the first signs that there is a stronghold of sin in your life that needs to be dealt with. Pouring out what God has poured into you never creates any measure of slothfulness.

**"Rejoice in hope, be patient in tribulation," (Romans 12:12a)**

It is in the hard times when the truth of your testimony will be the most apparent to others. Anyone can be happy when times are good. An atheist or an agnostic can and will rejoice during good times – but rejoicing in the difficult times requires being firmly anchored to the Lord of hope. To celebrate when God is good to you is wonderful, but the greatest testimony will be to rejoice in the hope that you have during a time of tribulation. When your life feels shattered, when it is dark, and all feels lost, take what is left of your broken heart and give it to God, for He heals the broken hearted and binds up their wounds.[48] In tribulation, your light will shine the brightest for the gospel. The Macedonian church once demonstrated this.

**"We want you to know, brothers, about the grace of God that has been given among the churches of Macedonia, for in a severe test of**

---

48    Psalm 147:3

**affliction, their abundance of joy and their extreme poverty have overflowed in a wealth of generosity on their part. For they gave according to their means, as I can testify, and beyond their means, of their own accord, begging us earnestly for the favour of taking part in the relief of the saints - and this, not as we expected, but they gave themselves first to the Lord and then by the will of God to us. (2 Corinthians 8:1-5)**

In the middle of a severe test of affliction, what little they had left was given to the Lord, and then by the will of God, it overflowed to others. Though they had little left spiritually, they lived lives with an 'abundance of joy.' Though they had little physically, they gave what they had to meet the needs of the saints. I'm not suggesting that God is commanding you to give every last penny you have to someone else. But I do believe that even in hard times, rejoice in the hope that you have, be patient, and continue to let the glory of God and the welfare of others be your primary focus.

**"Be constant in prayer." (Romans 12:12b)**

This is a commandment for both the good times and the bad as well. I don't think there is a clearer picture of what it means to not be conformed to the patterns of this world, but to be transformed by the renewing of your mind. Unceasing prayer does not produce godliness, but it is the first sign of genuine godliness. Continually come before God, and learn to share His heart for people in this world. Continually be conformed to His image as you learn to love the world the way He does. Come and attach yourself to Him – not to the ritual of telling Him what you need and want, but come to Him and seek *Him*. Seek *His* heart. Let *Him* be the focus of your prayer time, and let prayer be constant. What does it mean to be alive in Christ? It means to be in constant pursuit and communion with God, and there is no place this is better represented than in times of prayer.

**"Contribute to the needs of the saints, and seek to show hospitality." (Romans 12:13)**

Contribute not only to the physical needs of other Christians, but to their spiritual needs as well. Love each other as a church until the world can look at you and be persuaded that there must be something special about you just by the way you love each other. When other people have needs, do your best to help them. And when you have needs, do not be afraid to share them with other Christians. At the very least, you can pray for one anther's needs. Let all spiritual victory be hand in hand with other believers, and let no disunity in the church ever slow down the advance of the church against the gates of hell.

**"Bless those who persecute you; bless and do not curse them." (Romans 12:14)**

Living in Christ means loving people with a love greater than the love you can produce on your own. It means loving others in the way that God loved you. God came down, took the place of His enemies and died, and you ought to love others in the same way. Jesus died even for the men who beat Him, whipped Him and nailed Him to a cross, and He did it out of love for them. This kind of love is not something you can produce, but must flow from Him into you, and then into others.

**"Rejoice with those who rejoice, and weep with those who weep." (Romans 12:15)**

Love other people, because God has loved you! Does the creator of the universe not see and care for every tear you've shed? Does He snarl at you in hard times and tell you to man up? No, but He holds you and comforts you and walks with you while you weep. So also be to others a comfort and a caring shoulder for them to lean on in hard times. Continue to love them long after you think the mourning should have ended. Love people so completely and unconditionally, that regardless of what is going on in their life you are beside them. Love others so much that when they smile, you smile, and when they cry, your heart breaks with theirs. Is this not how Jesus has loved you?

**"Live in harmony with one another." (Romans 12:16a)**

It was Jesus who founded the church, and not people.[49] There is a reason why God gave us communion with other Christians – it is a tragedy when a church becomes merely a room full of Christians who listen to a sermon together, but do not share true fellowship with each other. Live in harmony with one another! Share each others' pain! Pray for each others' weaknesses! When you struggle with sin, the two greatest lies Satan will tell you are that God can stop loving and using you, and that you are struggling alone. You are never alone in your struggles – no temptation has overcome you that is not common to other people.[50] One of the greatest blessings of my time in high school was meeting with other believers in the library for a prayer meeting at lunch. One of the most beneficial things you can have in your spiritual walk is others with whom you can be vulnerable with, confess your sins to and pray with.[51] This is why prayer meetings are so important. This is why church is so important. And this is why vulnerability is so important in both.

**"Do not be haughty, but associate with the lowly." (Romans 12:16b)**

The truth about grace is that there is never a moment in your life where you don't deserve the wrath of God. But He has held back from crushing you because of His grace. If you really understood how poor you are before God, you wouldn't have a problem associating with the poor – both the physically and the spiritually poor. As God has treated you, so you ought to treat others. Were you not once bankrupt, sick, wounded, blind and dying? This is how you were spiritually, and God was not only willing to associate with you, but willing to adopt you as His son or daughter. How much more then, ought we be to those who are in the same state – both physically and spiritually?

**"Never be wise in your own sight." (Romans 12:6c)**

---

49      Matthew 16:18

50      1 Corinthians 10:13

51      James 5:16

It is always fundamental to understand that God's work depends on God and not on His people. You do have the responsibility to go, and to explain the gospel to others, and to disciple, but it is God's wisdom, flowing through you by His grace that will satisfy people's hunger for truth, and answer the questions that would draw them into maturity. It is not what you have to contribute. If you feel that you are wise, smart, and have a good understanding of all Biblical things, it is because you have become hardened and proud. If God is an eternal God, you will never come to an end of the things you can learn about Him. As long as you are seeking Him, there is not one part of His character He can not show to you in a new way. But it is always to the poor and the needy that Christ comes, not to the wise who feel they have everything together. It is to the humble that He gives grace, not to those wise in their own sight.

**"Repay no one evil for evil, but give thought to do what is honourable in the sight of all. If possible, so far as it depends on you, live peaceably with all." (Romans 12:17-18)**

God loves you, even when you don't love Him back. In the same way, let love and grace and mercy flow from you into others, even when you don't get it back. You are simply pouring out to others what God has poured into you. Do whatever you can to make past grievances right. Ask God to show you hindered relationships in your life, and what you can do to reconcile them.

**"Beloved, never avenge yourselves, but leave it to the wrath of God, for it is written, 'Vengeance is mine, I will repay, says the Lord.' To the contrary, 'if your enemy is thirsty, give him something to drink; for by so doing you will heap burning coals on his head.'" (Romans 12:19-20)**

You can avenge yourself in a variety of ways for wrong that has been done. You can avenge yourself with words, with actions, with the changing of a friend dynamic. You can avenge yourself just lying alone in your bed with cold thoughts toward a person. Do not avenge yourself, for if God had avenged Himself for every time you had sinned against Him, you would be long dead. Instead, love others, as He loved you. Not just because they get coals heaped on their head – or else that isn't love at all.

**"Do not be overcome by evil, but overcome evil with good." (Romans 12:21)**

This is at the heart of victorious Christian living. Learn and study the Bible so that you can understand who God is. When you begin to understand who God is, you will understand what good is, for His character is good. You are not to determine your own standards for right and wrong, but to look to Him to see the true definition of what is morally acceptable. The evil of this world will be overcome by your love – the shadows will be overcome by light. We don't overcome evil by resisting it, but by offence against it, and the weapon of our offence is love. When others hurt you, love them.

This is a small example of what it means to be alive in Christ. This is normal Christian living – loving and serving others with a love that could never be produced on your own.

And this is how you preach without words. Let your life be a testimony to the Saviour that has conquered sin and been raised again, giving new life. Actions speak as loudly as words – talk is cheap. Anyone can talk like a Christian – the greatest testimony to your faith will be living like one.

**"The aim of our charge is love that issues from a pure heart and a good conscience and a sincere faith." (1 Tim 1:5)**

Present your body as a sacrifice to God, and be transformed by the renewing of your mind – transformed into someone who does to others as God does to you. This is what it means to be dead to sin and alive in Christ.

*Dear Father,*
*You are good even when there is nothing good in me.*

*You bestow your riches when I am poor.*
*You have made me into a new creature,*
*and I want to live out that reality as a testimony to others.*
*Would you fill my heart with your love, that it might pour into others?*
*I know the good I ought to do, but I can not do it on my own,*
*It requires a transformation by your power,*
*Please fill me and pour out of me into others.*
*In Jesus name,*
*Amen*

## Chapter 10: Be Filled With the Spirit

The Holy Spirit. I don't believe there is a more disagreed upon, mistaught, misunderstood concept mentioned in the Bible. If you're familiar at all with various church denominations and their different teachings, a shudder ran down your spine as soon as you saw the title of this chapter. The Holy Spirit. He's overemphasized, and He's overlooked at the same time. There's a multitude of books written about Him, there's a multitude of books written against Him. The Bible says He gives gifts, but some people say He doesn't give gifts any more, or He doesn't give all the gifts anymore, or He gives gifts that are not mentioned in the Bible, or gifts are just a fancy way of saying we all have talents. Most evangelicals start their prayers with 'Dear Jesus,' or, 'Father,' but almost never pray to the Holy Spirit. Some charismatic churches don't pray to anyone but the Spirit. Some preachers say that every believer is filled with the Holy Spirit, others say everyone has the Spirit but isn't filled with Him, and others say only the apostles could have been filled with Him. I could go on. The point is that there are a variety of different opinions on who exactly the Spirit is and what He is like. So it is a little bit daunting to try and tackle this.

The Spirit is the third part of the Trinity. God the Father, God the Son (Jesus) and God the Holy Spirit are each individual persons, but are only One God. No analogy, no logic, no human intellect has ever been able to comprehend this concept. But there is no division, no dissension and no separation between the three parts of the Godhead. So God is only one God.

1 Corinthians 1&2 tells us that wisdom about God is foolishness to those of this age and in this world, for no one has seen or heard what God has in store for those who love Him. But,

**"These things God revealed to us through the Spirit. For the Spirit searches everything, even the depths of God. For who knows a persons thoughts except the spirit of that person, which is in him? So also no one comprehends the thoughts of God except the Spirit of God. Now we have received not the spirit of the world, but the Spirit who is from God, that we might understand the things freely given us by God." (1 Corinthians 2:10-12)**

This Spirit, that searches everything, even the depths of God, and is given to us so that we can understand the things freely given us by God – this Spirit was by the prophets. Isaiah described the Spirit, saying He would turn back the effects of fruitlessness, and establish justice and righteousness, resulting in peace.

**"For the palace is forsaken, the populous city deserted; the hill and the watchtower will become dens forever, a joy of wild donkeys, a pasture of flocks; until the Spirit is poured upon us from on high, and the wilderness becomes a fruitful field, and the fruitful field is deemed a forest. Then justice will dwell in the wilderness and righteousness abide in the fruitful field. And the effect of righteousness will be peace, and the result of righteousness, quietness and trust forever." (Isaiah 32:15-18).**

Isaiah promised it would be given some day, and you can see where Jesus described the Spirit in a similar way in John 14:16-17. In Ezekiel, God talks about changing man's heart, and putting within him a Spirit that will cause people to obey His rules.

**"And I will give you a new heart, and a new spirit I will put within you. And I will remove the heart of stone from your flesh and give you a heart of flesh. And I will put my Spirit within you, and cause you to walk in my statutes and be careful to obey my rules." (Ezekiel 36:26-27)**

And you can see Jesus describing the Spirit in similar ways in John 14:23-26. So the Spirit reveals to us things given freely by God, restores righteousness and teaches us to obey God's laws. Jesus spoke to the apostles about this Spirit after His resurrection, immediately before ascending into heaven, saying,

**"But you will receive power when the Holy Spirit has come upon you, and you will be my witnesses in Jerusalem, and in all Judea and Samaria and to the end of all the earth." (Acts 1:8)**

And, sure enough, just a few days later,

**"When the day of Pentecost had arrived, they were all together in one place. And suddenly there came from heaven a sound like a mighty rushing wind, and it filled the entire house where they were sitting. And divided tongues as of fire appeared to them and rested on each one of them. And they were all filled with the Holy Spirit and began to speak in tongues as the Spirit gave them utterance." (Acts 2:1-4)**

The Holy Spirit had come, and, filled with power, the apostles went to Jerusalem, and then to Judea, and then to Samaria, and the gospel has been headed for the ends of the earth ever since. You can read the book of Acts and see the host of miracles, conversions and divine appointments credited to the Holy Spirit. That book has often been incorrectly labelled 'The Acts of the Apostles.' It would more accurately be called 'The Acts of the Holy Spirit.' Peter and Paul, headed into the world, were never shy to bring news of the Holy Spirit with them, but believed all Christians should have a filling of the Spirit. According to the prophets it would restore righteousness and teach us to obey God's laws. No conviction of sin would come without a work of the Spirit.

And doing so was to fall right in line with the rest of the Biblical figureheads, who had all looked forward to a day when God's Spirit would come. From Moses[52] to Joel,[53] the forerunners of Christ had all been anticipating a day when God's Spirit would be poured out. At Pentecost the Spirit was finally poured out on Peter and the other apostles, who went into all the world preaching the good news with power.

**"And with great power, the apostles were giving their testimony to the resurrection of the Lord Jesus, and great grace was upon them all." (Acts 4:33)**

---

52      Numbers 11:29

53      Joel 2:28

They had power. They *needed* power – by every bit of human logic and reasoning, Christianity was doomed to failure from the start. Christianity's leader was known to have been publicly rejected and killed. Who would want to follow a man who couldn't save Himself? It wasn't long afterwards that the Jews began persecuting Christians, beginning with the stoning of Stephen.[54] By 54 AD, Nero, the emperor of Rome, was persecuting Christians by the droves. He would dress them in furs to have dogs tear them apart, or crucify them, cover them in tar and then burn them to light up his dinner parties. By human logic, no one in their right mind would walk the streets of Rome, look up at the torched body of a crucified man and say 'I want to be what he was.' No rational person could witness the bloody death of Christians, and say 'I want to become one of them.'

But the Holy Spirit was at work, speaking to the hearts of men about God's wisdom – a wisdom that was foolishness to man. And despite everything Satan threw at the church, the church continued to explode in growth. The persecutions came and went, depending on the emperor. Marcus Arelius and Diocletian were two of the cruelest, killing Christians in violent, torturous ways as public spectacles to the empire. Yet for every Christian that was torn apart by lions in the Colosseum it was as though ten men would stand up and say 'I want to be one of them!'

Christians were like seed – one would fall to the ground and die, and a whole crop would rise from that ground. Christianity exploded across the Roman empire, and over the course of only a few decades, thousands were converted. Why? Why would any logical, rational, sane human being want to join that number? Why would anyone even consider becoming a believer? Proclaiming faith in Christ, was, at times, like willingly joining death row. What rational human being would give up their life for such a cause? Why couldn't Christianity be stopped? Because the Holy Spirit had come. Jesus had promised the apostles power, and their words had such power that men were persuaded to believe.

---

[54] Acts 7

And it didn't stop in Rome. You would do well to go and read of the ways God has worked in revival in the past. The word revival seems to have lost its meaning recently, by being overused, abused and in many circles has become cliche. But revivals through history have been anything but cliche.

In 1741 Jonathan Edwards stood in Enfield, Connecticut and preached a sermon titled 'Sinners in the Hands of an Angry God.' He was not a great public speaker – by the light of a candle he held his notes a few inches from his face and read in monotone. People literally fell out of their chairs with conviction. He was interrupted several times by people crying out 'What must I do to be saved?' Stories are told of men clinging to the pillars of the church, fearing that they would fall straight into hell as the Holy Spirit penetrated their hearts and revealed their sin to them.

In 1949, Duncan Campbell arrived on the Hebrides Islands, just off the coast of Scotland. The first night he preached, was to a congregation of about 300. He stepped down from the pulpit, and as he walked away from the church, he met a young man praying and weeping for God to pour His water onto thirsty land. In a matter of moments, a blacksmith ran up to Mr. Campbell and called him to come back to the church to preach again. By the time he got back, it was almost 11:00 at night, and the small congregation of 300 had doubled . Over 600 people had gathered in the small church, seeking God and waiting for Mr. Campbell to speak. No one had planned a second meeting that night – people just spontaneously decided to come. A group of young people that night had been dancing at a local club when God suddenly began to move in their hearts. All at once, the entire dance floor evacuated as every young person fled and ran together to the church. They weren't the only ones running to the church that night – by the time they had finished singing a psalm, the church was filled with over 800 people. Where had they come from? From all over the island, all at once recognizing their need for God and running to His house in the middle of the night. Duncan Campbell preached until 4 am, seeing many converted. He continued to preach, day after day, all over the island under similar circumstances, and for the next 3 years, God continued to manifest His Presence in similarly extraordinary ways.[55]

---

55       Campbell, Duncan. "Revival on the Isle of Lewis." Sermon.

Bill Mcleod, the pastor of a Baptist church in Saskatoon, Saskatchewan had been praying for a work of God and promoting prayer in his church for years until he finally saw revival in 1971. Ralph and Lou Sutera, two travelling preachers began preaching on a Wednesday night meeting to a group of about 150 people. By Saturday, the building was too small to contain the crowds that were coming. Every night the meetings grew and people were converted in large numbers. In large numbers people were making their sins right with God and with other people. The chief of police issued a report saying that large numbers of people were coming to admit of past crimes and make things right. From Saskatoon poured a movement that carried around the world for years to come.[56]

Time and space would fail me to write of the many mighty moves of God that have taken place in the centuries since the church began. Here is a hurried synopsis of only three, and all took place relatively recently. Now consider your own churches, and contrast it with the power that flooded from the apostles, the early Christians in the Roman Empire, and other Spirit-filled men in history. Is the gospel that is being preached in this country preached with enough power that it would persuade men to join us, even if it meant certain death? The truth is that these works of God shouldn't actually be all that extraordinary. We do, after all, serve a God of the extraordinary. When we consider how God has worked in the past, and then look at ourselves, we ought to pray as Habakkuk did,

**"O LORD, I have heard the report of you, and your work, O ORD, do I fear. In the midst of the years revive it; in the midst of the years, make it known; in wrath remember mercy." (Habakkuk 3:2)**

Basically what Habakkuk is praying is 'God, we have heard of what you did in days long ago. Do tremendous things here again. I know you

---

Available at: http://www.sermonaudio.com/sermoninfo.asp?SID=5562

56 McLeod, Bill. "The Revival in Saskatoon Canada in 1971- a first hand report." Online Posting to *SermonIndex*. Web. Last accessed 16 Jun. 2013. Available at http://www.sermonindex.net/modules/newbb/viewtopic.php?topic_id=29901&forum=40&0

are angry with the sin of your people, but be merciful and come work here again.' And this, I believe, is the prayer of every hungry believer. The Spirit has done tremendous things in the past – persuading men to convert – pray that that same Spirit would fill your mouth with words of power!

There are many preachers that would suggest that the filling of the Holy Spirit received on Pentecost was sufficient for all believers for all time. Basically, 'Peter preached with power, and you have just as much power.' But I don't believe there is anything received by Peter or another apostle that is sufficient for me. Christ died as a sacrifice for Peter, and Peter received that gift, but Peter's acceptance was not sufficient for me – I, independent from Peter, needed to be cleansed by Christ. Jesus commanded that all men needed to be born again, but not one of the apostles had a second birth that was sufficient for any other human being of any age other themselves. There is no gift given in the New Testament to a believer, that I do not, today, need to reach out and take by faith for myself.

The Spirit promised by the prophets that came at Pentecost, is still offered to the believer today. Scholars might argue, but Scripture makes it clear, and I always take Scripture over scholars. The Spirit-filled life is available to the Christian today. He may not make Himself known in the same ways He did in Acts, or perform the same works in the same ways, but He is still here, still working, and still available. The Spirit-filled life is not an extra or abnormal thing, it is simply the way a Christian is supposed to be. We are commanded to be filled with the Spirit.

**"Do not get drunk with wine, for that is debauchery, but be filled with the Spirit." (Ephesians 5:18)**

The Spirit that grabbed hearts in Connecticut, Scotland and Saskatoon, can fill your heart too. And, just as the prophets foretold, it will lead you into righteousness, and teach you to obey God's laws. The Spirit will convict you of sin, for He is God, and God hates sin. As He fills you, He will lead you away from sin and into more righteousness.

"But I say, walk by the Spirit, and you will not gratify the desires of the Flesh." (Galatians 5:16)

"Now the works of the flesh are evident: sexual immorality, impurity, sensuality, idolatry, sorcery, enmity, strife, jealousy, fits of anger, rivalries, dissensions, divisions, envy, drunkenness, orgies, and things like these. I warn you, as I warned you before, that those who do such things will not inherit the kingdom of God. But the fruit of the Spirit is love, joy, peace, patience, kindness, goodness, faithfulness, gentleness, self-control; against such things there is no law. And those who belong to Christ Jesus have crucified the flesh with its passions and desires. If we live by the Spirit, let us also walk by the Spirit." (Galatians 5:19-25)

The fruit of the Spirit are not characteristics we are expected to try hard to produce on our own. Rather, they are what naturally flows out of the life of a Christian living in the power of the Spirit.

Almost every Christian believes in the Holy Spirit. Most would confess to believing that you can be filled by Him. But belief that doesn't create action has never done anyone good. You can believe in the power of the Spirit, but if you don't experience that power, what good is it to you? You can believe in the work of the Spirit, but if you don't want it and don't ask for it, what good is that belief to you? If you don't want something badly enough to pay the price for it, that desire will do you no good. You can want a Ferrari – you might even have enough money for one if you sold your house – but if you don't want it badly enough to pay the price for it, you'll never have it. So it is with the Spirit. Many people want the benefits of the Spirit, but they don't want to pay the cost. They don't want their life to be taken over by a Spirit. Being filled with the Spirit is primarily a handing over of control. It is taking the keys of your life, giving them to God and saying 'You can drive.' He rules your life – driving you away from sin and towards the life He wants you to have.

"For those who live according to the flesh set their minds on the things of the flesh, but those who live according to the Spirit set their minds on the things of the Spirit. For to set the mind on the flesh is death, but to set the mind on the Spirit is life and peace. For

**the mind that is set on the flesh is hostile to God, for it does not submit to God's law; indeed, it cannot please God." (Romans 8:5-8)**

The passage goes on to say that everyone has the Spirit – this is made clear elsewhere in Scripture as well. But there is a difference between having something and being filled with something. A glass can have water in it, but that does not mean it is filled with water. More than that, a glass can not be filled with something new, when there is something old in it. You can't fill a glass with milk if it is already full of water.

And so it is with the Spirit. You can not be filled with Him, until you are emptied of everything else. You may have Him – every believer does, but as time has worn on, self and sin may have crept in and taken up the corners of your heart, preventing the complete filling of the Spirit. He won't fill what He can't have, and He can't have what is filled with something else. If your heart is filled with a passion or a love for anything other than God, you can not be filled to the utmost with the Spirit until those things are dealt with, for they crowd Him out. It is paramount, if you want to be filled with the Spirit, that you must be emptied of other things. You can't have a great love for yourself, because a love of self will prevent you from handing yourself over to His control. You can't have a great love for anything material, for the Spirit is spirit, and not interested in things that are material. You can't have a heart concerned with romance or the future, good deeds or great accomplishments. The heart must be emptied of all things to make room for the Spirit.

The heart that wants to be Spirit-filled must be crucified again. The heart that wants to be filled with the Spirit must see all its desires brought to an end by the cross. The cross is a cold, hard, killing machine that puts to death everything that is on it. The cross has always been, and remains, the only way to any of the blessings of God. You must die to live. This is why faith in the finished work of the cross is the only pathway to God.

And once there is a filling – once there is a full handing of control over to God – once there has been a complete emptying of 'self,' the Spirit begins to lead the Christian completely. The Christian will find himself led away from sin, for he will no longer have a desire for it. He will feel great distress for worldliness of the church, the burdens of fellow believers, and the many lost souls all around him. He will find greater opposition than ever, being mocked by fellow Christians for trying to be too holy, by unbelievers for being insane and will be opposed by Satan, for a surrendered man in the hands of God is hell's greatest adversary. Spiritual usefulness will mark the life of the Spirit-filled Christian. When preaching, when sharing Christ with others, even just in ordinary acts of love towards other people, the very presence of the Spirit-filled Christian can be used to bring conviction to others. A Spirit-filled person may not have superior logic or tremendous oratory skills, but will have the Spirit of the Living God dwelling within them, guiding their every word. The sin-hating, righteousness loving God that loved the world, sent His Son and desires that no man should perish will flow out of everything that a Spirit-filled person does, so that their very words radiate with love and life. This is why Jonathan Edwards, Duncan Campbell and Bill McLeod can preach and see thousands flock to Christ – the Holy Spirit was filling their ministry. The gospel the Spirit-filled Christian preaches, comes with conviction, just as Paul's did.

**"Our gospel came to you, not only in word, but also in power and in the Holy Spirit and with full conviction." (1 Thessalonians 1:5a)**

Is that how the gospel comes out when you present it? Sometimes the best way we know how to defend Christianity is to look at worldly things. You point to various celebrities – athletes, movie stars or authors – and say, 'that person is a Christian! Look at the star player on this sports team, he is absolutely amazing, and he is a Christian.' We look at history and find great figures and say, 'Christian!' We look at political history and say 'our country is technically founded on Christian principles!' And? What good does any of that do? All it does is appeal to people's flesh. We would do far better to learn the power of the cross, and proclaim it not with anything appealing to the world, but simply by the power of the Spirit at work in us.

**"For I decided to know nothing among you except Christ crucified. And I was with you in weakness and in fear and much trembling, and my speech was not in plausible words of wisdom, but in demonstration of the Spirit and of power, that your faith might not**

**rest in the wisdom of men, but in the power of God." (1 Corinthians 2:2-5)**

A.W. Tozer once said, "You might satisfy the intellects of men by external evidences, and Christ did, I say, point to external evidence when He was here on Earth. But He said, 'I am sending you something better. I am taking Christian apologetics out of the realm of logic and putting it into the realm of life. I am proving My deity, and My proof will not be to a general or a prime minister. The proof lies in an invisible, unseen, but powerful energy that visits the human soul when the gospel is preached – the Holy Ghost! The Spirit of the Living God brought an evidence that needed no logic; it went straight to the soul like a flash of silver light, like the direct plunge of a sharp spear into the heart."[57]

When the Spirit fills your heart, your very life is a testimony that pricks the consciences of others and convicts people of their sin. Your words have power. The same power that persuaded Romans to join death row for the sake of Christ. Jesus had said,

**"But you will receive power when the Holy Spirit has come upon you, and you will be my witnesses in Jerusalem, and in all Judea and Samaria and to the end of all the earth." (Acts 1:8)**

When He said it, He wasn't kidding. And He wasn't speaking to the apostles exclusively. I don't ever want to undermine the sovereignty of God – I believe the church has stepped into great error when it tries to bring about God's work by itself – but often we take an overly passive approach in seeking a work of God. God is in control. God is sovereign. God will work in His time, in His way. But this does not exclude your duty and your privilege to actively seek an outpouring of God's Spirit. It is like a farmer that must diligently plough the field, plant the seeds and watch over the crop. God alone can send rain, and God alone can make seeds grow. But do not be the kind of farmer that sits around and waits for fields to plant themselves.

---

[57] Tozer, A. W. *How to be Filled with the Holy Spirit.* Mansfield Centre, CT: Martino Publishing, 2010.

Seek the Spirit. Seek to have Him fill your heart. Seek His work in your life. Martin Lloyd-Jones once wrote, "The prescription is this - seek Him! Seek his love, seek his life, seek to know him in the very vitals of your being; seek that you may be filled with love to Him, and you will receive the gifts. Not talking about them always, not having meetings about them. No! Have meetings about Him! Preach about Him! Seek Him! Love Him!"[58]

This isn't some sort of abnormal or strange life, but one mandated by Christ and the rest of the Scriptures. The first time Satan ever deceived someone, he began with the question 'Did God really say?'[59] And he hasn't changed a bit. I believe He is very quick to cast doubt wherever and whenever He can. It would seem he has heaped a multitude of doubt onto every passage concerning the filling of the Holy Spirit for post-New Testament believers. 'Did God really say that was for you?' The Bible commands us 'Be filled with the Spirit.' Do not doubt that this passage comes from God – it is as reliable as every other word in the Book.

Much has been done in the name of the Holy Spirit that is abnormal, strange, extra-Biblical, and so forth. But this is no reason to shy away from Him. Much has been done in the name of Christianity that is false – yet we know there is legitimacy to our gospel despite all the times it has been maligned. Do not look at a misuse of the Spirit as a reason for you to ignore Him.

The Spirit is God. He is part of the Trinity. He is not any less God than the Father is. He is equal in the Godhead with Jesus. As such, He possesses every characteristic and every attribute of God, for He is God. He doesn't act in a way that is different than how the Father would act, for they are the same. Someone can not claim to be filled with the Spirit and be doing things that are contrary to God's nature. That is contradictory. A person filled with the Spirit will not be led by

---

58    Lloyd-Jones, Martin. *The Sovereign Spirit*. Wheaton, IL: Harold Shaw Publishers, 1985. Print.

59    Genesis 3:1

the Spirit to do things that Jesus would not do, for Jesus and the Spirit are the same essence.

I'm not concerned about the specifics of what it looks like to be filled with the Spirit. I'm not concerned with which gifts are relevant, or which denomination has gotten things right. You can read the Bible for yourself and decide whether all the gifts are still being given or not. And when you encounter crazy things happening in churches, you can pray and study the Bible for yourself to discern whether or not what you are seeing is genuine. I will only point you to this verse,

**"Do not quench the Spirit. Do not despise prophecies, but test everything; hold fast what is good." (1 Thessalonians 5:19-21).**

The Holy Spirit inspired the Bible. He will reveal Himself to you through it. If you disagree with anything I've said, or you want to know more, study the Bible for yourself. The Spirit is all throughout the Scripture, although I specifically recommend looking at 1 Corinthians. The most important thing in the studying of the Spirit is to not elevate experience above Scripture. Scripture is the final authority. If you come from a cessationist (Holy Spirit gifts have ceased) background, and don't believe in the work of the Spirit because you have never seen it – please, study the Scripture and don't let your own experiences interpret the truths of God's Word. Let it speak for itself. And if you come from a charismatic background and believe everyone should speak in tongues or be praying to the Spirit or whatever, please, don't let what you are accustomed to interpret the Bible. Let it speak for itself. I wouldn't go so far to say that either of those parties is wrong. I will just point all of you that are reading this to the Bible and encourage you to build your understanding of the Holy Spirit on His Words about Himself, and not on your experience.

Study the Bible, and seek the Spirit. Ask God for the Spirit. He is willing to give Him to you. He wants to give Him to you!

**"If you then, who are evil, know how to give good gifts to your children, how much more will the heavenly Father give the Holy Spirit to those who ask Him!" (Luke 11:13)**

According to the words of Isaiah, He will restore peace and righteousness. According to Jeremiah, He will teach you to obey God's commands. According to Jesus and the accounts in Acts, He will give power that convicts of sin. Seek the work of the Spirit.

> There are riches in Thy storehouse,
> But my Lord we are so poor,
> There is power in Thy storehouse,
> But the cripple clothes our door.
> There is wisdom in Thy storehouse,
> But thy people are so bound.
> There is glory in Thy storehouse,
> But it does not shine around.
> There is love within Thy storehouse,
> But Thy people are so dry.
> There's compassion in Thy storehouse.
> Then, my Saviour, why, oh, why
> Are Thy people stony-hearted
> And our eyes so desert dry?
> -Leonard Ravenhill[60]

*Dear Father,*
*You have promised the gift of the Spirit to those who ask,*
*and you have commanded us to be filled with the Spirit.*
*Father, I surrender the entirety of my life to your will,*
*Lead me and control me by your gentle Spirit.*
*Seek out the things in my life that fill my heart instead of you.*
*Reveal yourself to me, reveal your power in me,*

---

[60] Ravenhill, Leonard. *Heart Breathings.* 'In Thy Storehouse.' Available at: http://www.ravenhill.org/heartb8.htm

*Like Habakkuk, I have heard of your work in the days of old*
*Work mightily here again Lord, in wrath remember mercy.*
*Send a revival Lord, start the work in me.*
*In Jesus' name,*
*Amen.*

## Chapter 11: Dying to Live

Christ died, and if you are a Christian, His death was your death too. Everything that you are – all your sin and all your self was put on the cross and killed with Christ. You died.

And then Christ rose from the dead. He not only forgave sin, but He conquered it, and His resurrection was your resurrection too. All the power that overcame sin was given to you. He rose from the dead and He made you a new creation. A new person, with new desires, and a new heart. You must die to live.

**"Having been buried with him in baptism, in which you were also raised with him through faith in the powerful working of God, who raised him from the dead. And you, who were dead in your trespasses and the uncircumcision of your flesh, God made alive together with him, having forgiven us all our trespasses." (Colossians 2:12-13)**

But as time wears on, and the pressures of life crowd in, sin and deadness crawl back in. You were raised to life, but you begin to sleep, spiritually, resembling all the dead men around you. And when this happens to Christians, we just become a valley of dry churches. Like the valley of dry bones that God breathed upon and raised to life, we need the breath of God to come and fill us again, stirring us to new life, raising us into an army.

It's time to lay down sin, to lay down the love of ourselves - our own dreams, desires, ambitions and pleasures and to take up God. To learn to love God with all our heart, soul, strength and mind, and to love our neighbours as ourselves. Its times for the church to seek intimacy with God, seek holiness, and seek the Spirit. I will be greatly disappointed if what is written here does not drive you into a deeper study and desire for the Scriptures. I hope that what is written here is not seen as a foundation to build a Christian life upon, but something that helps to tip you farther into the study of the Bible – the Book that will truly give you something to build a Christian life upon.

We live in a day when a vibrant, passionate Christian life is an abnormal thing. Though the world may scorn you, though the church itself may mock you, my prayer is that you, who are reading this, will lay down everything that you are, take up your cross and follow Christ. For the past several months I have been praying that *you*, who are reading this, will go into school, the workplace, the neighbourhood, into whatever regular swing of life you have, and proclaim the truth of Christ's cross to all who you encounter. May you live every moment of your life as a testimony to God's power.

What does it mean to live in Christ? Love God. Love others. How do you do that? By His power working through you.

Are you dying to live? Lay down sin. Lay down self. Take up Christ. Every day, for the rest of your life.

**"And [Jesus] said to all, 'If anyone would come after me, let him deny himself and take up his cross daily and follow me." (Luke 9:23)**

Be dead to sin, alive in Christ.

> O Lord, we labor in a day
> When men of faith are few.
> Now just a remnant watch and pray.
> Again we beg – endue
> They Church with apostolic power
> For true revival in this hour.
>
> Have we the holy channel blocked
> With unbelief and sin?
> Have we not asked and sought and knocked
> To bring the Glory in?
> How is now Thy Spirit grieved

That He withholds the shower
That would revival tide bring in,
And apostolic power?

Is Thy blest holy Word unread?
Have we but ceased to pray?
Have carnal longings in our hearts
Brought spiritual decay?
Come, Thou great Physician, come,
And circumcise the heart;
Fleshly impediments remove,
And all Thy might impart.
-Leonard Ravenhill[61]

*Dear Father,*
*You have called me to be a soldier.*
*Crucify me again.*
*Show me how to live the new life you have given.*
*Teach me that you are all that matters in my life.*
*Give me an unquenchable desire for you.*
*Teach me how to be holy.*
*Draw near to me as I draw near to you.*
*Teach me about yourself, and all the you give.*
*Let me live a life that proclaims your truths.*
*Fill me with your Spirit.*
*In Jesus name,*
*Amen.*

---

[61] Ravenhill, Leonard. *Heart Breathings.* 'Thy Glory.' Available at: http://www.ravenhill.org/heartb8.htm

"Now to him who is able to keep you from stumbling and to present you blameless before the presence of his glory with great joy, to the only God, our Saviour, through Jesus Christ our Lord, be glory, majesty, dominion, and authority, before all time and now and forever. Amen."

**(Jude 24-25)**

In addition to the works that are directly referenced within the book, this is a list of resources that were influential in the writing process. Themes, ideas and lessons were borrowed from each of these works, and credit is due.

I thoroughly recommend each book and sermon listed here as a resource to further your study on any of these topics.

### Chapter 1: We Are Soldiers

Ravenhill, Leonard, *Why Revival Tarries.* Bethany House Publishers, 1986. Print.

Ravenhill, Leonard. "Judgement Seat of Christ." Sermon. Available at: http://www.sermonaudio.com/sermoninfo.asp?SID=922020713

### Chapter 2: My Own Funeral

Cymbala, Jim *Fresh Wind Fresh Fire.* Grand Rapids, MI: Zondervan, 2003. Print.

Tozer, A.W. *The Radical Cross.* Camp Hill, PA: Wing Spread Publishers, 2009. Print.

Ravenhill, Leonard. "Spirit of a True Prophet." Sermon. Available at: http://www.sermonaudio.com/sermoninfo.asp?SID=510032540

### Chapter 3: A Living People

Washer, Paul. "Modern American Christianity." Sermon. Available at: http://www.sermonindex.net/modules/mydownloads/singlefile.php?lid=12827&commentView=itemComments

### Chapter 5: You Don't Have It Because You Don't Want It

Blackaby, Henry. *Experiencing God.* Nashville, TN: Broadman & Holman Publisjers, 1998. Print.

Edwards, Jonathan. *The Life and Diary of David Brainerd.,* Public Domain.

Ravenhill, Leonard. "Desperate Prayer." Sermon. Available at: http://www.sermonaudio.com/sermoninfo.asp?SID=11602172059

Tozer, A.W. *The Pursuit of God*. Harrisburg, PA: Christian Publications, Inc., Copyright MCMXLVIII. PDF Document.

**Chapter 6: You Want Me To Look Like What?!**

DeYoung, Kevin. *The Hole in Our Holiness.* Wheaton, IL: Crossway, 2012. Print.

Greening, Mark. "Revival Now." Sermon. Available at: http://www.sermonindex.net/modules/mydownloads/singlefile.php?lid=19844&commentView=itemComments

Spurgeon, Charles. *All of Grace.* Public Domain.

Tchividjian, Tullian. *Jesus + Nothing = Everything.* Wheaton, IL: Crossway, 2011.

**Chapter 7: The Torn Veil**

Armstrong, Arnie, and Amy Hancock. *The Lord Has Spoken.* Victoria, BC: self-published, 2007. Print.

Carre, Captain E.G. *Praying Hyde.* Alachu, FL: Bridge-Logos, 2011. Print.

Piper, John. *Desiring God.* Sister, OR: Multnomah Publishers, Inc., 2003. PDF Document. Available at: http://dwynrhh6bluza.cloudfront.net/resources/documents/5154/bdg.pdf?1321962222

Tozer, A.W. *Paths to Power.* Camp Hill, PA: Christian Publications Inc., publishing date unknown. Print.

Tozer, A.W. *The Pursuit of God*. Harrisburg, PA: Christian Publications, Inc., Copyright MCMXLVIII. PDF Document.

**Chapter 8: Giving Back**

Carson, D.A. *A Model of Christian Maturity*. Grand Rapids, MI: Baker Book House Company, 2007. Print.

Murray, Andrew. *The Deeper Christian Life.* Print Basis: Fleming H. Revell, 1895. Kindle File.

**Chapter 10: Be Filled with the Spirit**

Campbell, Duncan. "Revival on the Isle of Lewis." Sermon. Available at: http://www.sermonaudio.com/sermoninfo.asp?SID=5562

Finney, Charles G. *Lectures on Revival.* Minneapolis, MN: Bethany House Publishers, 1988. Modified ed. of *Lectures on Revivals of Religion.* 1835. Print.

Lloyd-Jones, Martin. *The Sovereign Spirit.* Wheaton, IL: Harold Shaw Publishers, 1985. Print.

Murray, Andrew. *In Search of Spiritual Excellence – Discover Power-filled Living!* Springdale, PA: Whitaker House, 1984. Print.

Tozer, A. W. *How to be Filled with the Holy Spirit.* Mansfield Centre, CT: Martino Publishing, 2010. Print.

Tozer, A.W. *Keys to the Deeper Life.* Grand Rapids, MI: Zondervan, 1973. Print.

Tozer, A. W. *Tragedy in the Church: The Missing Gifts*. Harrisburg, PA: Christian Publications, Inc., 1978. Print.

Tozer, A.W. *Paths to Power.* Camp Hill, PA: Christian Publications Inc., publishing date unknown. Print.

Kevin Deane
is an author, actor, preacher, camp-goer and coffee lover.
You can email him at KevinDeane93@gmail.com
Follow on Twitter: RealKevinDeane
Check out the blog on his website:
http://valleyofdrychurches.webs.com/